THE BEST PU
NORTH WALᴸᴸᴶ

ALSO BY MIKE DUNN

The Penguin Guide to Real Draught Beer

Birmingham Pubs 1880–1939
(with Alan Crawford and Robert Thorne)

Local Brew

The Best Pubs in Lakeland

Walking Through the Lake District

Walking Ancient Trackways

The Lake District

THE BEST PUBS IN

North Wales

Mike Dunn

Illustrated by Phil Evans

ALMA BOOKS

IN ASSOCIATION WITH THE
CAMPAIGN FOR REAL ALE

Author: **Mike Dunn**

Design: **Opus**

Cover photograph of the Vaynol Arms, Nant Peris: **Morris, Nicholson, Cartwright Ltd.**

Cartography by: **Perrott Cartographics**

Typeset and printed by: **Cambridge University Press**

ISBN **1-85249-102-7**

Published by **Alma Books Ltd.**, *a wholly-owned subsidiary of the Campaign for Real Ale Ltd., 34 Alma Road, St Albans, Herts.*

© *Mike Dunn/Alma Books Ltd 1989/90*

CONTENTS

ACKNOWLEDGEMENTS

The compilation of this guide, covering such a large area of the country, has been a mammoth task. It has been made much easier, however, by the contributions of others, and my thanks go to all of them, including Philip Levison, for his superb coverage of Anglesey; Ian Ogden and Pete Zemrock, for their comments and information on much of Clwyd; Alan Banks and Kevin Gamble, for their contributions on northern Clwyd; Richard Andrew for details of pubs in the Aberconwy area; Huw Rees for a cracking suggestion in Powys; Jill Adam and Mark Enderby for oiling the wheels; and last but not least Neil Harris, for his general encouragement and his emergency dash to the wilds of Glyndwr. Thanks are also due to those landlords who good-humouredly (for the most part!) answered my questions, and provided the beer and in some cases the accommodation: with particular thanks to Les Gallagher for his hospitality. Finally, special mention should be made of the home team, Chris, Katie and Sarah, who displayed their usual forbearance — within limits!

MIKE DUNN

INTRODUCTION

The prospect of researching this guide sounded too good to be true — a tour of North Wales in search of the very best pubs that this spectacularly scenic part of the country (defined here as Clwyd, Gwynedd and the northernmost part of Powys) can offer. A vision quickly came to mind of inviting seashore hotels, timeless country locals nestling beneath craggy cliffs or with glorious views of the Snowdonian mountain ranges, and classic town pubs cheek by jowl with medieval castles.

It *was* too good to be true, of course. There are indeed some pubs like that, but it quickly became clear that for every one of those there are a dozen which are decidedly not worth seeking out. Some of these are ordinary locals, admirably fulfilling their basic purpose but without any particular attraction for visitors to the area. Far too many others are simply unappealing: garish town locals, especially in the beer deserts of the north coast resorts, and in the bigger towns; village inns where just about everyone — including the landlord — appears hostile to newcomers; country pubs which are cold, dirty, and (worst of all) inexplicably closed. One rural pub which springs all too easily to mind had no beer to speak of, no food at all, no facilities for families, and an overgrown garden boasting the battered and unsafe remnants of a children's swing and two rickety picnic tables literally on their last legs.

All this sounds pretty depressing, and it's intended to do just that. I now adhere firmly to the view that there are more bad pubs per square mile in North Wales than almost anywhere else in Britain. But there is better news too: I also discovered some of the best pubs in the world here, and quite a few more which should be on every serious beer drinker's itinerary (and they're all in this book!).

THE PERFECT PUB

More generally, my good, bad and indifferent experiences in scores of North Walian pubs led me to draw up a checklist of factors worth bearing in mind by serious drinkers looking for the perfect pint in the perfect pub. Perhaps the first essential point they should bear in mind is that North Wales is big – very big. It therefore contains a remarkable variety of landscape and culture, and its pubs reflect this with a diversity of architectural and social styles which is staggering. It soon becomes clear that the quest for the perfect pub involves more than simply seeking out mountain hotels idyllically situated at the foot of spectacular peaks in the middle of Snowdonia.

This is just as well, since the second essential point is that there are, regrettably and mysteriously, precious few decent pubs in Snowdonia itself. In the mountain fringes there are splendid country pubs such as the Olde Bull at Llanbedr-y-Cennin, snugly situated in the northern foothills of the Carneddau, and remarkable unspoilt boozers like the Douglas Arms in Bethesda, but the mountain fastnesses have precious little to offer the pubgoer.

The third golden rule (again hedged with exceptions!) is to avoid the North Wales coast and to look slightly further inland for decent beer in decent pubs. Close to (and usually just to the south of) the A55 expressway right across North Wales there are excellent pubs far more deserving of your support than the brash seaside town pubs. To take a few examples: the Britannia at Halkyn, still with a farmyard atmosphere yet providing excellent meals too; the Rock at Lloc, a wonderful wayside inn and as comfortable a venue for relaxed drinking as could be imagined;

the Swan at Llanfair Talhaiarn, a notably welcoming village pub; and the Ty Gwyn at Roewen, above the Conwy valley.

Even the most fastidious of drinkers would find it hard to criticise pubs such as these, amongst the cream of the area's hostelries. The excellence of others is, perhaps, more open to debate. No selection can hope to satisfy everyone, since virtually every pub has its supporters and most – however intrinsically appealing to the casual visitor – have their detractors too. But the pubs chosen for inclusion represent an unbiased, honest attempt to identify the very best pubs, of whatever style, in the whole of North Wales.

Every pub we've included has real ale, of course; whilst it can sometimes disappoint, it is almost invariably superior to its keg rivals, weighted down by the crushing mediocrity of processed beer, and occasionally it is magnificent. Every pub, too, has a warm welcome for visitors. In addition, almost all provide acceptable bar food (and many do much better, with a commitment to really appetising food which is to be applauded); the exceptions tend to be the more traditional, unspoilt rural pubs which are included for their unchanged character rather than their culinary pretensions.

Many of the pubs in this book have accommodation on offer, though prospective overnight guests should be warned that this varies from ensuite bedrooms in rather smart hotels to basic though still adequate bed-and-breakfast in country inns with only one or two letting bedrooms. Not that there is anything second class about some of the inns in this second category. I defy anyone to find better value-for-money than the Red Lion at Cyffylliog near Ruthin, with excellent Lees beer in addition to *very* reasonable rates for a comfortable bed for the night and a really substantial breakfast.

And then there are the waterfront pubs, like the Gazelle on the Menai Strait (admittedly more expensive but still good value), the fishermen's inns of the Dee valley, the coaching inns in towns such as Bala and Corwen....

Not everyone wants good food and accommodation, of course, and the guide also seeks out the very best traditional drinkers' pubs – pubs where the quality of the beer counts for much, though naturally the general ambience is of importance too. Pre-eminent amonst these pubs is the White Lion at Pen-y-Mynydd: it's wonderfully unchanged despite the nearness of Chester, which seems to have influenced a disproportionate number of nearby pubs to transform themselves into steak houses and theme pubs, to the detriment of local drinkers. Lovingly run by three sisters, and with due regard paid to the real ale, the old-fashioned atmosphere and the art of unhurried conversation, the White Lion is a must for visiting pubgoers. Few better pubs will be found in these pages.

LOST PUBS AND BREWERIES

Sadly, other pubs which might have been included for similar characteristics are not here because their life as a pub has drawn to a close. The Jenny Jones on the outskirts of Llangollen is one such, remembered with affection by many. With respect to the other pubs in that tourist trap of a town, the Jenny Jones was in a class of its own, beautifully unspoilt and with that all-too-rare timeless feeling. In the hard-nosed commercial world, however, it could not provide a sufficient return on assets. The Plough at Llanrhaedr-ym-Mochnant is a similar, though more recent, casualty; a classic rural pub with a cast-iron stove, it exuded warmth and character. Whilst a return to the old days, when even a little town like Llanfyllin had 43 alehouses, is neither feasible nor desirable, the gradual erosion of the country's stock of outstanding unspoilt pubs is potentially disastrous. Taking the trend to its logical extreme, only the larger outlets will survive outside town centres – and then mostly as Beefeaters, Harvesters, Toby Grills and the like. The brewers, preoccupied with making their assets sweat, might want that; but do we?

Not only pubs are being closed. The stock of traditional breweries is equally under threat – together with the highly individual beers that many of them produce – as corporate greed is translated into takeovers and closures. Soon there could be just a few "national" breweries producing identikit beers, and a mere handful of small traditional brewers, denied access to wider markets and thus meeting only very local needs. Even today hardly a drop of real ale is produced in the whole of North Wales. The number of independent brewers in the region has slowly declined, with Wrexham's nineteenth-century brewers gradually whittled away and the coastal brewers swallowed up by their more powerful competitors. Greenall's, for example, owe their presence in Clwyd mainly to the purchase by the Chester Northgate Brewery (later to become part of Greenall's empire) of the Kelsterton Brewery Company and its 93 pubs in 1899. Burtonwood, too, have expanded via takeovers, the biggest being that of Lassell & Sharman of Caergwrle, with 50 tied houses, in 1945.

The final blow was the takeover of Border Breweries of Wrexham by Marston's in 1984. Though the brewery was somewhat rundown, distinctive beers were produced there and some investment (or takeover by a company which, like Burtonwood, had pledged to keep the brewery open) could have rescued the situation. As it was, Marston's quickly closed down the brewery, and though the names of the beers survive they are now brewed in Burton-on-Trent.

The new brewery revolution which has swept

over most of Britain, with over 200 new ventures since the late 1970s, has largely left North Wales untouched, with a few brave but ultimately unsuccessful ventures and only one remaining new business. Gwynedd Brewery in Anglesey tickled local palates for a while with beers like Snowdon Strong; Cestrian Brewers of Buckley similarly failed to stay the course; and even the brewery at the City Arms at Minera near Wrexham, set up by Allied Breweries, and quickly establishing a reputation for tasty beers, has been closed down. Only Plassey Brewery near Wrexham, whose Farmhouse Bitter is unfortunately very difficult to track down, is still actually making beer.

FOREIGN BEERS

A saving grace for North Wales drinkers is that quite a number of excellent beers from faraway brewers find their way into the area. Pre-eminent amongst these, perhaps, are Marston's beers, found not only in the former Border Breweries pubs but also in Marston's existing North Wales tied estate and a thriving free trade. Another notable contribution is made by the Manchester brewers, several of whom diversified away from their north-western base, especially in the inter-war period. As a result beers from Robinson's, Burtonwood and Lees are all well represented in this guide. Honourable mention should also be made of Banks's, whose tied houses touch only the southern and eastern fringes of the region but whose good-value beers are becoming quite widely available.

The bad news is that the icy grip of the national brewers is very strong in North Wales, especially in the coastal resorts. Many pubs tied to the big brewers now provide some real ale, but its quality is generally lower than that of the smaller brewers. Curiously, despite all their advantages the big fish find it possible to brew only a few distinctive beers between them. Too many pubs are thereby severely restricted in the choice of worthwhile beers they can offer drinkers; and too many more, so-called "free" houses, are guilty of similarly tying themselves to the inferior products of the big boys. Discerning drinkers still have to vote with their feet in too many areas; and only optimists have yet seen signs that the aftermath of the Monopolies and Mergers Commission's report will improve the situation.

REAL ALE

A recurrent theme of preceding paragraphs has been the availability of real ale, and much has been made of its virtues. It might therefore be worth explaining what it is, and why it's worth searching for. Essentially it is beer which has been brewed, stored and served in the traditional manner. At the brewery it is brewed from natural ingredients – malted barley, hops, yeast and water. Once fermented it is racked into casks, primed with a little sugar in order to encourage a secondary fermentation, and left to mature; this conditioning, so essential to the development of subtle flavours, is cut short in keg beers by chilling, filtering and pasteurisation.

In the pub the beer is very often served by beer engine – the common-or-garden hand-pump – which is a comfortingly familiar sight on most bar counters nowadays. Occasionally the beer may be poured direct from the cask "by gravity", though this is uncommon in North Wales except with strong ales such as Old Tom in Robinson's pubs. Some rural locals such as the Queen's Head at Ty Croes on Anglesey, the Goat at Llanfihangel-yng-Ngwynfa in deepest Montgomeryshire and the Three Pigeons in the Vale of Clwyd still use gravity dispense for all their beers. A third alternative is for the beer to be drawn out of the cask by electric pump, as in the Hydes pubs near Wrexham and some Banks's and Robinson's outlets.

Keg beers and British lagers, on the other hand, already with much of the goodness taken out by chilling and filtering (and in any case quite often brewed from inferior materials), are further chilled in the pub and then pushed from the keg by carbon dioxide pressure. The low temperature and high gas content serve to mask the lack of flavour. The result is pure liquid mediocrity – a clear, fizzy and virtually tasteless concoction.

MILD AND BITTER

Real British beer, however, though it may occasionally disappoint (usually because either the brewer or publican has cut corners), still has a wide variety of styles and at its best is a superb, palate-tingling experience. The basic draught styles are bitter, usually light-coloured, and mild, usually much darker (though there are darkish bitters which are actually a good deal darker than many light milds such as Robinson's Best Mild!). Bitter, though, is the great British beer, although there is enormous variation from one part of the country to another and even between different breweries in the same town. The sweeter beers of the Midlands, for example, contrast sharply with the subtle, bitter beers of the south-east and the smooth, creamy north-eastern bitters. Equally there are differences in colour, from light straw-coloured bitters to golden, reddish and even maroon hues. And there is a gradation from low gravity "boy's bitters", weak but sometimes refreshing and ideal quaffing ales, through standard, medium-strength beers to the top-of-the-range premium bitters and strong ales. In North Wales very good ordinary bitters are provided by Banks's and Lees amongst others. Stronger beers include Marston's Pedigree, though the strongest available are the famous and unusual Theakston's Old Peculier, with its peculiar spelling and very peculiar effects on some, and two marvellous draught barley wines, Marston's Owd Rodger and Robinson's Old Tom.

Mild ale has been in decline for many years now, hampered by its cloth-cap image and also, perhaps, by its generally less distinctive taste (less well-hopped and therefore characteristically somewhat blander than bitter, and also a little weaker on average). Nevertheless there are some excellent milds remaining, and Burton-wood's creamy Dark Mild is not a bad example, though it is in by no means all of their pubs in North Wales. Regrettably, their excellent Light Mild is no longer brewed. Marston's Merrie Monk, occasionally available in one or two of the pubs in this book, is amongst the strongest in the country and has a unique taste.

These, then, are the best beers to be found in the best pubs in North Wales. Tourists here for the mountains of Snowdonia, the beaches of Lleyn or Llandudno, the fortresses of Harlech, Conwy or Caernarfon, or the scenic splendours of areas like the Dee valley, the Vale of Clwyd or the Menai Strait might see them as useful halting places for a lunchtime meal or a reflective drink after sundown. More bibulous visitors can easily construct a whole tour around them: after all, the scenery is still there after closing time!

HOW TO USE THIS GUIDE

The guide is divided into the three areas of Clwyd, Gwynedd and northern Powys. The pubs are listed alphabetically according to the town or village in which they are situated (or, if isolated, the nearest centre of population). The practical details for each pub are given in the left-hand column, and symbols are used to give the following information:

 food is available as specified. This always means full meals; other pubs without the symbol may well serve snacks. Many pubs do not serve meals late in the evening, so check by phone if you wish to eat late.

 a garden or other outdoor area for drinking – occasionally this will just be tables on the pavement.

 a family room or area without a bar is provided where the licensee will allow children accompanied by a parent or other responsible adult. In pubs where meals are served children may be confined to the dining area, and thus be expected to have a meal. Check with staff.

 the type of accommodation ranges from three-star hotels which sell real ale to more modest pubs with bedrooms or self-catering facilities. No prices are given. Check by phone for availability.

 real ales are listed with beers from independent breweries given first, followed by the generally inferior national brands. For full details of beers see the brewery section on page 19 or consult CAMRA's Good Beer Guide.

PUB HOURS

In August 1988 the Government finally made long-overdue changes to pub licensing laws, which had been severely restricted since the First World War. Pubs can now open on Mondays to Saturdays from 11 am to 11 pm. However, individual licensees can choose which hours they wish to open within those limits. They will choose their hours to suit their trade. Since many are still experimenting, the details for individual pubs are still subject to change, and we have therefore not included details here. But it is reasonable to anticipate that pubs in urban areas and tourist areas will stay open in the afternoons, especially in the summer, while remoter pubs may take advantage of the new laws only on Fridays and Saturdays, if at all. Many pubs display their opening hours outside the pub; it is confusing (and deplorable) that not all pubs do so.

WELSH SUNDAYS

Sunday hours have been only slightly extended: the standard hours are now 12 noon to 3 pm and 7 pm to 10.30 pm. This of course applies only where there *are* standard hours on Sundays; for in Wales, uniquely and anachronistically, Sunday opening is subject to a referendum every seven years. The most recent, in November 1989, saw residents in Anglesey and eleven other "wet" districts, as well as in the two hitherto "dry" ones of Arfon and Ceredigion, forced to vote on the question of seven-day opening. All except Dwyfor voted for Sunday opening, usually by very substantial margins. It really is time for this ludicrous and tiresome business to be brought to an end.

CHILDREN IN PUBS

You cannot drink alcohol in a pub below the age of eighteen years (although at sixteen, children with adults may drink beer, cider or wine with a meal). You can go into a pub at fourteen but only to drink non-alcoholic products. Licensees tend to be extremely strict on "under-age drinking" since they can be prosecuted and lose their licences to trade. Children of all ages can, however, go into pubs that have rooms set aside as "family rooms". They can also eat in pubs that have rooms used as restaurants. If a pub in this guide is shown to have a beer garden then children can use this facility, though if the garden is reached via the pub it is wise for parents or guardians to ask permission to take the children through the licensed area.

THE BREWERS

Although, with one tiny exception, there are no surviving independent breweries in North Wales nowadays (indeed, the only brewery in production is that of the former Wrexham Lager Beer Company, now part of Allied Breweries and still producing lager only) beer drinkers in the region still enjoy an excellent choice of real draught beers. This is in large measure due to the wide spread of beers from the independent brewers in the Manchester area – such as Robinson, Lees and Burtonwood. In addition to this Marston, although they reduced choice virtually overnight when they bought and then closed down the Border Breweries plant in Wrexham in 1984, produce a commendably wide choice of real ales, and have vastly increased the number of ex-Border pubs serving a decent pint.

On the other hand, it has to be recognised that the drinking pleasures of North Wales are limited in some respects. The most potent limiting factor is the very wide spread of pubs owned by, or otherwise tied to, the bigger brewers, and therefore condemned for the most part to selling the insipid products of these far from quality-conscious combines. And the position has worsened in recent years, with Greenall's closing their excellent Wem brewery in 1988 – it was always a mystery how such a traditional brewery was able to survive as a subsidiary for so many years – and Boddington's selling their breweries to Whitbread in 1989. At least this second blow will have only a limited effect in the Principality, though the handful of pubs selling beers from Boddingtons' subsidiary company, Higsons, will doubtless find themselves obliged to change brews when Higsons gets the almost inevitable chop.

What follows is a full list of the real ales which – barring further disasters – can be tasted in the best pubs in North Wales, with a description of the brewer, the beer name, its original gravity, and a comment (inevitably subjective) on the style and quality of the beer. The original gravity figure – for example 1040 – is a good guide to strength and, when compared with relative prices, of the value-for-money of different beers. Essentially it is a measure of the amount of raw materials used in brewing the beer, as a proportion of the amount of water used. Thus a 1040 beer comprises 40 parts of fermentable material to 1000 parts of water. The weakest beers brewed tend to have a gravity of 1030 or so; 1037 is an average strength for ordinary bitter; 1040 to 1045 covers most strong bitters; and 1070 to 1080 strong ales and barley wines.

ANSELLS

See Ind Coope.

BANKS of Wolverhampton

One of the biggest but paradoxically one of the very best of the independent breweries, Wolverhampton & Dudley Breweries (trading as Banks and Hanson) has some 800 pubs, mainly in the West Midlands but with a few in south-east Clwyd and a handful around Machynlleth. Good, cheap beer in pleasant surroundings is virtually assured.
MILD ALE (1035) Medium dark, with a mellow, nutty flavour.
BITTER (1038) An excellent bitter, dry and crisp and with a noticeably hoppy aroma.

BASS of Burton-on-Trent , Birmingham, Cardiff and Sheffield.

The beers come from various trading companies in the massive Bass organisation.
M & B MILD (1036) A run-of-the-mill mild.
WELSH BREWERS HB (1037) A smooth ordinary bitter.
STONES BEST BITTER (1038) A pale bitter, surprisingly well-hopped and refreshing.

M & B BREW XI (1040) Remains sweet and unspectacular despite attempted improvements. DRAUGHT BASS (1044) Still one of the better beers from the big brewers, but sadly only a pale shadow of the once-great brew.

BODDINGTONS of Manchester

An ambitious company, once regarded as amongst the most traditional of brewers. Took over Oldham Brewery (now closed) and **Higsons** in the 1980s, then stunned the brewing world by selling its breweries to Whitbread in 1989. Now anything could happen to the beer and the Strangeways Brewery.
BITTER (1035) Nothing like the distinctive pale, sharp bitter which was revered in the 1970s.

BURTONWOOD of Burtonwood

A family-controlled brewery with 290 pubs, over a third of them in North Wales as a result of takeovers from the 1930s onwards, notably of firms in Caergwrle, near Wrexham, and Ewloe.
DARK MILD (1032) Creamy and smooth, popular with many.
BITTER (1036) Well-balanced and pleasant, occasionally outstanding.

FELINFOEL of Llanelli

One of the smaller surviving brewers, yet well known for its quality beers.
BITTER (1035) Pleasant and light, very rarely seen in traditional form yet, astonishingly, on sale at the Sun in Rhewl near Llangollen.
DOUBLE DRAGON (1040) An excellent full-flavoured premium bitter, widely available in the free trade.

GREENALL'S of Warrington

The biggest independent brewery company in the country. Has recently closed down its breweries at Wem and Birmingham.
MILD (1034) Dark, malty and unassuming.
BITTER (1037) Unmemorable.
THOMAS GREENALL'S ORIGINAL (1045) Much better than the so-called "Original" which was

introduced in 1983 and subsequently withdrawn, this one is meaty and quite powerful! The best from Greenall's for some time.

HIGSONS of Liverpool — A sad story. Higsons was a well-regarded local brewery which sold out to Boddingtons in 1985. Now that Boddingtons in turn have sold the breweries to Whitbread, the future of Higson's beers must be precarious.
MILD (1032) A malty dark brew.
BITTER (1037) Well-hopped, unusual and very popular locally.

HYDES of Manchester — The smallest and in many ways the most endearing of Manchester's surviving independent companies, still brewing two different milds at the Anvil Brewery. Inexplicably has seven pubs in the Wrexham area, detached from its main tied estate.
MILD (1032) Low-gravity but well-regarded and still with a deliciously malty taste at its best.
BITTER (1036) Well-balanced and with a strong local following.

IND COOPE of Burton-on-Trent — A subsidiary of the giant Allied Breweries. Also brews Ansells beers amongst many others.
ANSELLS MILD (1035) Dark, malty and with a rather cloying palate.
ANSELLS BITTER (1037) Too sweet for many tastes.
IND COOPE BITTER (1037) Hoppier than in the past but of no great distinction.
BURTON ALE (1047) One of Allied's very few noteworthy real ales, Burton Ale is strong and distinctive, with a refreshingly hoppy taste.

LEES of Manchester — Another family-controlled independent from the Manchester area, without the reputation of others but with beers worth sampling.
GB MILD (1032) A pleasant dark amber brew. The initials are those of Lees' Greengate Brewery.

BITTER (1038) Much-improved; creamy and light.
MOONRAKER (1074) Relatively recently introduced on draught, a heavy, malty and dark barley wine.

McEWAN of Edinburgh

Part of Scottish & Newcastle, as are **Theakston** and **Younger**.
70/— (also sold as YOUNGER'S SCOTCH) (1036) A dull, sweetish, middle-of-the-road bitter.
80/—(also sold as YOUNGER'S IPA) (1042) Heavier but still bland.
YOUNGER'S NO. 3 (1043) A dark ale with a proud history.

MARSTON of Burton-on-Trent

A major regional brewery with pubs from Cumbria to Hampshire following a series of takeovers, including that of Border Breweries in Wrexham in 1984 to increase its presence in North Wales. Brews a very wide range of real ales.
BORDER MILD (1031) A weak, inoffensive and sometimes very pleasant dark brew.
MERCIAN MILD (1032) A surprisingly full-flavoured and by no means sweet beer.
BORDER BITTER (1034) A clean-tasting light brew.
BORDER EXHIBITION (1034) A rare medium mild, well worth seeking out.
BURTON BEST BITTER (1037) A fine ordinary bitter, a splendidly refreshing brew which is highly regarded.
PEDIGREE (1043) Advertised as "the king of bitters" and rightly so: this is a full-bodied, pale and delicate premium bitter. Subtly-flavoured and quite strong, it is one of the best bitters in the country.
MERRIE MONK (1043) A highly unusual strong dark mild, rich and sweet but otherwise not too dissimilar to Pedigree.
OWD RODGER (1080) A magnificent draught barley wine, very dark, rather sweet, rich and satisfying.

**MITCHELLS &
BUTLERS**

See Bass.

POWELL of Newton

Originally brewers from the 1880s onwards, then beer wholesalers, then brewers again since 1983, producing distinctive beers for a widespread free trade.
ORIGINAL (1038) Well-balanced and full of taste.
SAMSON (1050) A malty and powerful premium ale.

**ROBINSON of
Stockport**

An expanding Greater Manchester brewery which farsightedly bought a series of North Wales pubs in the 1930s and so is well represented from the English border right across to Anglesey. Robinson's beers are available in these pubs as well as quite extensively in the free trade.
BEST MILD (1032) Surprisingly pale, malty and full flavoured.
BEST BITTER (1041) A great bitter, very pale indeed but well-hopped and with a delicate but distinctive flavour.
OLD TOM (1080) One of the very few classic draught strong ales still with us, this is a dark brew, which is smooth but not too sweet, at its most popular in winter.

RUDDLES of Oakham

Formerly a proudly independent real ale brewer, now a subsidiary of Grand Metropolitan, the owners of Watney, Webster & Wilson amongst others.
BEST BITTER (1037) A standard bitter.
COUNTY (1050) A once-great beer which has lost character in recent years.

**JOHN SMITH of
Tadcaster**

The northern arm of Courage, now owned by Elders IXL, the company run by Australian tycoon John Elliott.
BITTER (1036) A fairly pleasant session beer.

SAMUEL SMITH of Tadcaster

A very traditional brewery which keeps faith with Yorkshire Squares for fermentation, wood casks for maturation, dray horses for local deliveries, and has real ale in all 300 pubs.
OLD BREWERY BITTER (1039) A very malty and quite dark brew, highly individual and too sweet for some.

TETLEY of Leeds

Yet another subsidiary company, this time (like Ind Coope) part of Allied Breweries.
MILD (1032) A noticeably malty brew, dark and rather thin-tasting.
BITTER (1035) Regarded as one of the better northern bitters, but with rather less flavour than some of its competitors; nevertheless a creamy and well-balanced brew.

THEAKSTON of Masham (North Yorkshire) and Newcastle

A famous Yorkshire brewery which sadly surrendered its independence to Matthew Brown in 1984, only to find itself part of Scottish & Newcastle as a result of a further outbreak of merger mania.
BEST BITTER (1037) A pale and still distinctive ordinary bitter.
OLD PECULIER (1057) Named after the eighteenth-century Peculier of Masham, brewed from a mash including malt extract, caramel and maize, but also dry-hopped to add a touch of bitterness. Slightly weakened in recent years, but still a unique strong dark ale.

THWAITES of Blackburn

A strongly traditional Lancashire brewery, renowned for its superb mild ales.
BITTER (1036) Well-hopped but not especially distinctive.

WEBSTER of Halifax

The northern brewery of the Watney/Grand Metropolitan combine, which since the closure of Wilson's Manchester brewery in 1986 has also tried to "match" the latter's beers.

WILSON'S ORIGINAL BITTER (1036) Well-balanced but without distinction.
WEBSTER'S YORKSHIRE BITTER (1036) A bland, utterly unmemorable brew.
WEBSTER'S CHOICE (1045) A somewhat fuller-bodied premium bitter.

WELSH BREWERS

See Bass

WHITBREAD of Castle Eden, Cheltenham and Sheffield

Castle Eden is one of Whitbread's very few remaining traditional breweries, and its future has been in doubt for years. Cheltenham now produces most of the traditional beers for the group, while Sheffield is best known for its keg beers.
TROPHY (1036) A very ordinary session beer.
FLOWERS IPA (1036) Dull.
CASTLE EDEN ALE (1040) A pleasant though rather sweet bitter.

WILSON

See Webster

WOOD of Wistanstow, Shropshire

One of the more successful new small brewers, started in 1980 next to the Plough Inn in the little village of Wistanstow near Craven Arms.
PARISH BITTER (1040) An extremely refreshing, hoppy and pale-coloured brew.

YOUNGER

See McEwan

ABERGELE
Harp

Tel: (0745) 824080
Market Street (A548)

✖ lunchtime and (summer)
 evenings

🍴

🍺 Boddingtons Bitter; Higson
 Mild, Bitter

Abergele, though somewhat overwhelmed by seaside suburbia these days, remains a pleasant enough market town, though its best feature lies a little to the west – Gwrych Castle, a romantic folly with eighteen turrets and castellation dating from as recently as 1814. The Harp, though hardly as picturesque, is an excellent town pub, vibrant, cheerful, bursting with character, and often bursting at the seams with customers. It has a 200-year history as a pub, but the building is much older: in the thirteenth century it was in use as the town's jail, and this role continued until its eighteenth-century conversion to a more convivial purpose. There's now a quite sizeable bar and two delightful lounge areas around an old inglenook fireplace and kitchen range. A friendly atmosphere pervades the place, not least on market days (when the Harp stayed open all day even before the advent of the new licensing laws). Higson's beer is a rare treat in North Wales, and following the Liverpool firm's sad demise – it was taken over by Boddingtons in 1985 – the parent company's bitter has also appeared on the bar. How long for is another matter, following Boddingtons' sell-out to Whitbread in 1989.

ACREFAIR
Duke of
Wellington

Tel: (0978) 820169
Llangollen Road (A539)

✖ lunchtime and evening

◎

🍴

🍺 Marston Border Mild, Border
 Bitter, Pedigree

A popular and very well-run former Border Breweries pub on the edge of an industrial village, but one with Llangollen and the Dee valley close at hand, and the spectacular Pontcysyllte aqueduct even closer. The old Llangollen canal also runs very close to the pub, which has a tiny bar, a side room with a darts board, and an award-winning garden to one side, with swings and an old farm tractor for children to clamber over. The bar has a number of outsize wooden spoons, one of them inventively used as a sports trophy, and a roaring log fire. The varied selection of racing photographs

on the walls – Lester Piggott included – testifies to the enduring popularity of the sport
amongst the regulars, who can usually be found
scattered around the bar, with its selection of
benches and stools around wrought-iron tables.
Sport features very strongly in bar conversations,
and there are keen darts, dominoes and football
leagues centred here. There's good solid pub
food, with generous portions, and apparently
there's even a singing dog. As for the Pontcysyllte
aqueduct, this spectacularly spans the Dee
valley at a height of 127 feet, its iron trough
carrying the Shropshire Union Canal across the
valley for 1,000 feet. The 19 cast iron arches look
particularly impressive from below, while the
towpath alongside the canal offers an unusual if
somewhat challenging walk (best undertaken
before a visit to the Duke of Wellington!)

BERSHAM
Black Lion

Tel: (0978) 365588
Off Bersham Road (B5099)
OS312492

Hydes Mild, Bitter

The Black Lion, known locally as the Hole in the
Wall, has been carefully modernised without
losing its essential character as a village local
relying largely on regular custom, now somewhat supplemented by the more adventurous
visitors to the Bersham Industrial Heritage
Centre, which is only a few hundred yards along
the road. Well worth a visit, the Centre – on
the site of the Wilkinson family's eighteenth-
century ironworks – explains the former importance of ironmaking in the area, based on the
ready availability of coal, iron and water power.
It is worth noting, though, that Bersham had
witnessed industrial development before that,
with the Croes Foel Smithy providing some of
the finest wrought iron gates in Britain. The Black

Lion, down below the B5099 in the pleasant hamlet of Ddol, has a typically functional main bar, a pool room to one side, and a small back room which serves well as a comfortable overflow drinking area. Coal fires provide a warming atmosphere in winter. Outside there are a few tables in a patio area to the front of the pub, facing the tiny lane which runs down from the main road.

The Black Lion,
Bersham

BODFARI
Dinorben Arms

Tel: (074 575) 309
Off A541

✗ lunchtime and evening

◎

▣

◲ Thwaites Bitter

Most first-timers are left speechless at the Dinorben Arms, an extraordinary seventeenth-century pub accompanied by an even more amazing garden, which comes complete with fountains, an astonishing array of flowers, and a covered terrace with its own 'Nook and Cranny', a little alcove with one table and two benches wedged inside. The pub itself is heavily half-timbered, and the tiered structure looks as though it is ready to put to sea. There is a variety of bars and restaurants, including the Badger Suite, which offers eat-as-much-as-you-like farm-house buffets on Wednesdays and Sundays, and a carver board on Thursday, Friday and Saturday evenings: the prices are high but then so is the food consumption! Families are welcome in the Garden Room, and beyond the massive tiered car park, with its one-way traffic system, there is a children's play area. The garden and verandahs have a fine view not only across the northern Vale of Clwyd but also of Bodfari's church tower rising above the timbers of the pub. Real ale is inevitably a bit of an afterthought but nevertheless it's a nice touch that it should not only be included in the many and varied attractions on offer but should also be an unusual beer for the area, and from an excellent brewery at that.

BRYMBO
Black Lion

Tel: (0978) 758307
Railway Road (off B5101)

▣

◲ Burtonwood Dark Mild, Bitter

Very much a bright spot in a pretty devastated industrial landscape, complete with railway viaduct, massive steel works and depressing waste land, the Black Lion is a busy community pub with an attractive rear bar and a delightful, cluttered front bar beloved of the racing fraternity. Once inside, the atmosphere is almost that of a country pub. A plethora of sports trophies decorates the shelves above the bar counter, while still more are in a case behind the bar. A fierce black lion hangs over the bar, standing guard over a row of glasses attractively stamped with the pub's name, all separately identified as the property of one of the regulars by a series of coloured pigeon rings, or in one case a silver sixpence, around the handle. The back bar has a few bar stools, a wood-panelled wall behind a settle which looks somewhat ill-at-ease in its surroundings, and lots of room devoted to darts and pool. Games are taken *very* seriously here: the ladies darts team (which must be a trifle difficult to beat) boasts two Welsh internationals. Sightseers are relatively rare, though the area is full of interest to the industrial archaeologist, and also has a certain charm for those fascinated by the remarkable contrasts in this little area of industrial villages between mines and tips, grim villages with austere chapels, and pockets of farmland and woods dotted with upmarket bungalows.

BURTON ROSSETT
Golden Grove

Tel: (0244) 570445
Llyndir Lane, Burton Green.
OS 354586

✖ lunchtime and evening

🍴

🍺 Wilson's Original Bitter;
Webster's Yorkshire Bitter,
Choice

Rossett, in the lowlands where the River Alyn prepares to join the Dee, is a border village with two corn mills – one black-and-white, dating from the fourteenth century, and the other eighteenth-century brick. Burton Green, away from the main road (but with the rumble of traffic on the by-pass fairly evident), is an area of scattered development with the Golden Grove standing some distance apart from the hamlet itself. It is an unusual pub, apparently dating from around 1234 and commonly regarded as an old coaching inn, though the reason for stagecoaches passing this way is somewhat obscure. Its remoteness is clearly seen as a selling point, for there are no signposts in the country lanes, and no inn sign on the building itself. The purpose of the big black-and-white building is unmistakable, however, and inside there is the snug cheeriness of a truly old pub, with low ceilings, open fires and an assortment of ancient-looking furniture. Families are allowed inside, and there is plenty of seating outside too, with an adventure playground for the kids and barbecue facilities for their parents. There is plenty of bar food, together with high quality cuisine from the full à *la carte* menu in the restaurant. It's a shame that all the beers come from one Big Six brewer even though the Golden Grove is a free house; but that's the sort of detail which might possibly change....

BYLCHAU
Sportsman's Arms

Tel: (074 570) 214
Bryntrillin (A543 three miles south-west of the village)

✕ lunchtime and evening

☺

🏠

🍺 Lees GB Mild, Bitter

A splendid hostelry remotely situated some 1500 feet up in the high moorlands of Mynydd Hiraethog, the Sportsman's Arms (Tafarn y Heliwr) claims to be Wales's highest pub, and there seem to be few counter-claimants. The sense of isolation is remarkable – it is eight miles to the village of Pentrefoelas in one direction, and nine to Denbigh in the other. All around are the moors and the wooded slopes of Clocaenog Forest, though the lapping waters of Llyn Brenig, man-made and of recent origin, bring a welcome diversity to the scene. There are also forest walks and picnic sites in the vicinity. The Sportsman's has a small bar and a much larger, comfortable lounge with a delightfully traditional atmosphere. There are also two restaurants, with an enviable reputation for good food – though good beer is also accorded proper priority. Although it is much favoured by tourists in the summer, the pub also performs a valuable function as a community centre all year round, with strong connections with local clay pigeon, hunting and sheepdog societies. And there's live entertainment on a regular basis, together with somewhat less formal but nonetheless appreciated outbursts of Welsh singing at weekends.

CARROG
Grouse Inn

Tel: (049 083) 272
On the B5437

✗ lunchtime and evening

⋈

🍺 Lees Bitter

People remember their favourite pubs for all sorts of reasons – because of the beer, the food, the landlord, the atmosphere, and a hundred other factors. But I suspect that those who number the Grouse at Carrog amongst their favourites will be unanimous in their opinion: the dramatic view. The most popular spot in the pub must be the window seat in the bar, looking out over the River Dee at its most majestic, flowing under the delightful old five-arched bridge which carries the B5437 towards the A5 and Llangollen. The bar itself, classically simple and unchanged for years, with horse brasses and a few old tables, sums up the pub, which is a totally unspoilt cottage-style inn dating from the early nineteenth century, with a few bedrooms and straightforward but appetising bar food amongst the facilities offered. Also available is pool, somewhat incongruously played in a room with a beamed ceiling, while to the side of the bar there is a small sitting room for private conversations. Another, rather more unusual, service provided by the Grouse is the sale of newspapers on Sunday mornings. Despite the pub's name, fishermen rather than crackshots dominate in the bar, and walkers too find the Grouse an ideal touring centre.

CILCAIN
White Horse

Tel: (0352) 740142
Off the A541

✗ lunchtime and evening

🏠

🍺 Sam Powell Samson; Ansells
    Bitter, Ind Coope Burton Ale

Two fading signs featuring a sad-faced horse and the long-defunct Chester Northgate Brewery advertise the White Horse at Cilcain, a classic village pub much appreciated both by the villagers and by the many walkers attracted to the nearby Moel Fammau, with its collapsed Jubilee Tower, and the other local beauty spots. A third white horse surmounts a creeper-smothered wooden structure by the lounge entrance. The lounge is a lovely small room with old beams, brasses, a copper-topped bar, an inglenook fireplace and very, very low seats.

Several cosy drinking areas lie beyond arches and steps away from the bar itself. The public bar, approached from the side entrance, is splendidly old-fashioned, with a quarry-tiled floor; it houses an impressive collection of more than a hundred bottled beers from all over the world. Excellent bar meals, including Norwegian prawns, several curries and very filling steak-wiches are served at lunchtime and until well into the evening. A true community pub, the White Horse (like the Grouse Inn above) acts as newsagent on Sundays, and is also the base for several clubs, including the local mountain bike fanatics. It's the only survivor of five pubs in the village, once home to spar and lead miners but now essentially a dormitory village; the Red Lion is now the post office, the Tyn Llan a guest house, and both the Crown and the Cross Foxes have become smallholdings.

CONNAH'S QUAY
Old Quay House

Tel: (0244) 812667
Dock Road (off A548)

✗ lunchtime and evening

🛏

⌘ **Greenall's Mild, Bitter**

Two roads lead to the Old Quay House – the narrowing Dock Road, passing under a low railway arch, and Quay Lane, even narrower and leading under an even lower arch. Between the two is another old railway track, this time disused and converted into a pleasant walkway heading for unexpected parkland on the other side of the traffic-infested A548. Beyond the pub are the sheds of the extravagantly named Quay Business Park, with Connah's Quay power station behind. But this unpromising beginning is misleading; the Old Quay House is worth the trip. The pub, right opposite the old quay, is a remarkable survival. A substantial whitewashed building, bearing the date 1777, it can hardly have changed in the last few decades. The boisterous heart of the place is the public bar, old-fashioned and quarry-tiled, and having as its centrepiece a bagatelle table (the game is still played very seriously here, and there are regular knock-out tournaments). The bar also has an excellent series of photographs showing the devastation wreaked by man along the banks of the Dee in the vicinity, together with studies of local river life; there is a piano with fishing nets draped on the wall above it. The atmosphere is tremendous; that in the smoke room to the side, and a lounge/dining room (and beer garden) at the back of the pub, approached through a big gateway (and not always open), is much more restrained.

The White Horse at Cilcain

Sir Gawain & the Green Knight

Golftyn Lane (500 yards from A548 jct)

✗ lunchtime and evening

🍽

☺

🍺 **Samuel Smith Old Brewery Bitter**

An unusual beer for the area and a bit of an oasis in a near-desert for real ale. The "Sir Gawain" (one wonders what the locals call the place?) is an old farmhouse now marooned in housing estates, converted and extended with Sam Smith's usual good taste to form a pleasant, easygoing pub with two interconnecting lounge bars. Locals tend towards the right-hand bar, with its bench seating, little bar stools and low tables; it's lively and cosmopolitan, but rather disrupted by a prominent television set. First time visitors might prefer the other end of the pub, its splendid stone fireplace flanked by ornate log baskets. Also here are some excellent prints giving an insight into brewing at Sam Smith's, Yorkshire's oldest brewery, including a reproduction of an oil painting of "Barrel", reputedly Sam's best dray horse, and an excellent photograph of the cooper's shop at the Old Brewery, with a wooden cask in the process of being repaired. The food is well-regarded locally, with Sunday lunch especially good value and evening meals available until half-past eight. The pub is also very handy for a recuperative drink for the more energetic after their exertions at the nearby sports centre. Outside there's a family beer garden with the usual play equipment, and a little patio raised above the car park at the front of the pub.

CORWEN
Owain Glyndwr

Tel: (0490) 2115/2407
The Square (A5)

✗ lunchtime and evening

☺

🛏

🍺 **Lees Bitter**

Formerly the New Inn (and hardly new, since it dates from the thirteenth century), the Owain Glyndwr was renamed in honour of the most illustrious of the Welsh princes, who held sway over most of Wales between 1405 and 1415, and bravely, but ultimately unsuccessfully, challenged the English empire-builders. Much later, in 1789, the inn achieved further distinction by hosting the first ever Welsh National Eisteddfod.

Now, imposing and handsome, it stands in the centre of the little town of Corwen, with its brown-shuttered windows, hanging baskets, and solid porch whose columns have carved capitals representing the Prince of Wales feathers. Above the porch is the sight which greeted the Reverend Richard Warner in 1797: "on passing through the town we were struck with a fierce, gigantic figure, which rose as a sign over the inn of the place. We found, on enquiry, it was the representation of Owen Glendower, whose memory is revered at Corwen". The tiny bar, with an attractive fireplace and a variety of pennants, is the natural focus of the place and is much favoured by the locals; get there early to claim a seat! The conversation turns quickly to farming, fishing and shooting, though much of it is in Welsh. The lounge, through a low-beamed archway towards the back of the pub, is relatively plain but has a piano as well as a food servery; there is also a separate restaurant. Children are especially welcome, and vegetarians too are well catered for. In the churchyard immediately behind the Owain Glyndwr are a number of gravestones which, following a local custom, have two hollows for the knees of those who come to pray.

CYFFYLLIOG
Red Lion

Tel: (0824) 6664
Three miles from the B5105.
OS059577

✗ lunchtime and evening

◎

ﾑ

ﾑ **Lees Bitter**

A small village four miles west of Ruthin, near the head of the Clywedog valley, Cyffylliog is too easily dismissed as having nothing of interest, but is in any case too far from the beaten track to attract many visitors. This is a pity; the village lies in charmingly unspoilt countryside, with the valley sides pressing in and the road running pleasantly through woodland, while the Red Lion is a marvellous unspoilt village inn, catering exactly as it should for the hungry, those in need of a bed for the night, and those who are simply thirsty. The food is substantial and excellent value; the breakfasts are especially memorable. The bedrooms are simple but again are good value. The beer, in the plain public bar, the pool room or the two-part lounge bar, is well-kept Lees (though keg and cask versions are available side by side: insist on the real stuff!). The lounge, with its low beamed ceilings, and little steps calculated to unnerve, is no place for the outrageously tall, but has a warming open fire, bench seating and tall bar stools, and a rather nice picture of the pub itself on one wall. A feature of the dining room, right at the back of the pub and with views of the wooded hillsides around the village, is an intricately carved low sideboard.

CYMAU
Olde Talbot

Off A541. OS297562

✕ lunchtime

◎

🛏

🍺 **Hydes Mild, Bitter**

The Olde Talbot, one of a cluster of seven pubs near Wrexham which through some quirk of history find themselves belonging to Hyde's Anvil Brewery from Manchester, lies on the edge of the little village of Cymau – so near the edge, in fact, that sheep graze just outside the windows from time to time. The village is largely a commuter settlement nowadays but has an interesting industrial past, while the countryside in this part of the Wrexham urban fringe is surprisingly attractive, well wooded and full of little hills and hollows. The pub sits on the top of one of the hills and so there are wide views across the little valley of the Alyn, especially from the road which climbs steeply from the A541 just north of Cefn-y-Bedd. The pub itself, a low whitewashed building on a bend in the road as it approaches the village, is essentially a village local with a delightfully relaxed atmosphere. The bar is largely frequented by keen games players – the rattle of dominoes is by no means unusual – and the rather smaller lounge is comfortable and more sedate, but is certainly an ideal venue for a peaceful pint. The food is simple but appetising and very good value, and the Hydes bitter a treat (try the mild as well, though there may be those in the bar who will try to deter you!).

CYNWYD
Blue Lion

Tel: (0490) 2106
On B4401

⊖ Marston Border Mild, Border Exhibition

Stone-built and rambling, hemmed in on one side by the old stables and on the other by a little lane, the Blue Lion is an uncompromisingly traditional pub in brown and cream, its little porch decorated with hanging baskets and the eponymous lion on the end gable but otherwise presenting a stern face to the world through its latticed windows. It is a good community pub, friendly and at times noisy, with a pool room and, in what is best described as an old-fashioned smoke room area, lots of horse brasses and an atmosphere sometimes as lively as that in the bar. Bitter drinkers are out of luck; the only real ales are two milds, including the rare Exhibition, arguably the best of the old Border Breweries' not especially lamented beers. What makes Cynwyd unique in the known universe, however, is that the other pub, the **Prince of Wales** across the road, also sells real mild only, in this case from Burtonwood. Seekers after unspoilt pubs will want to try this one as well as the Blue Lion: cramped, basic and parochial, with stone-flagged floors, presumably only its remoteness has ensured its survival in such an unchanged state.

DYSERTH
New Inn

Tel: (0745) 570482
Waterfall Road. OS055796

🕮

🍺 Marston Mercian Mild, Burton
Best Bitter

Just down the road from Dyserth's beauty spot, the little limestone gorge with its surprisingly impressive waterfall, and in consequence liable, apparently, to become flooded after heavy rainfall, the New Inn is a quaint survival of a type of pub which was once a great deal more common. Relatively ancient and with many small rooms, it is warmed by real fires and decorated with brasses. The Marston's beer is generally pretty good, too. Lively and popular, the New Inn boasts Welsh singing at the weekends and a Sunday night fun quiz which brings in the locals. The frontage is superb, with the long, low pub at right angles to the road, and a few benches in a rapidly narrowing front yard. Across the road is the troublesome brook, which once provided the power for a number of mills, all now disappeared, and also the heavily-restored parish church of Dyserth, a large sprawling village too close for comfort to both Rhyl and Prestatyn. To the rear of the pub is a pleasant, well-used and rather secluded beer garden. Old, interesting and homely, the New Inn is well worth a visit from those marooned in the Rhyl area. The more historically-minded might combine it with a visit to the site of the ill-fated Dyserth Castle, built in 1241 and destroyed by Henry III only 22 years later.

Red Lion

Tel: (0745) 570404
Waterfall Road. OS055793

✗ lunchtime

🕮

🛏

🍺 Greenall's Bitter

Sandwiched between the A547 Prestatyn to Rhuddlan and A5151 Holywell to Rhuddlan roads, and not far from the A55 expressway either, the Red Lion is nothing if not easy to get to. It is conspicuous in its local environment too, a big white-painted Victorian building right opposite the little car park provided for those visiting Dyserth's waterfall. It has a separate public bar and an interesting lounge with a large collection of plates and other ceramic memorabilia. Mainly populated by older pubgoers, especially in the winter months, the Red Lion is (like most of the local pubs) much busier in the summer, with tourists from Rhyl and Prestatyn contributing to a lively, uninhibited atmosphere. The younger regulars are often to be found in the games room, and there are also quiz teams based here. An even younger clientele frequents the beer garden, complete with children's play area, at the rear of the pub. The beer may be only Greenall's but it is well presented, and the lunches are locally popular; the Sunday lunch in particular is highly regarded and in consequence heavily subscribed. Right across the road are the waterfalls, an unexpectedly spectacular feature cascading down the limestone cliff, and there are also exhilarating if somewhat steep walks in the scenic countryside nearby.

FFYNNONGROEW
Garth Mill

Tel: (0745) 560141
Garth Lane (off A548)

🏚

🍺 Younger Scotch

An unusual pub in an unlikely setting, along a rough, narrow lane off the A548 close to the Llanasa turning. The lane leads to a shallow ford on the little Afon Garth; there is space to park on either side of the stream, and a footbridge for those unprepared to wade through. Built in 1743 as a corn mill, the Garth Mill's main purpose was to help feed the horses and pit ponies from the many lead and coal mines in the area. The mill ground its last corn in 1956 – defeated by the closure of the lead mines and the increasing mechanisation of the coal industry – but was neatly converted to a pub in the early 1980s (though a little faith is needed in recognising it as such – there's no inn sign). Now there is a delightful bar in the imposing three-story building, with ivy climbing right to the eaves and wooden shutters. The bar has two distinct sections, one (closest to the bar counter itself) low-ceilinged, intimate and convivial, and beyond a fine open fireplace a further comfortable lounge area taking full advantage of the height of the main mill building. On the walls around the bar a series of fascinating photographs documents the story of the mill and its conversion. Outside there is a sizeable beer garden with rough-hewn logs forming benches overlooking the stream.

GLYN CEIRIOG
Glyn Valley Hotel

Tel: (069 172) 210
At the junction of the B4500 and B4579

✗ lunchtime and evening

◎

ㅂ

🍺 **Marston Pedigree; John Smith Bitter**

Enterprising and lively, the Glyn Valley Hotel is right in the centre of the sprawling village of Glyn Ceiriog. The green-painted signs (which actually advertise Greenall's ales) create an expectation of Lees' beers; but while these were sold here some years ago, the real ales now come from Marston and John Smith. Remarkably spacious, the Glyn Valley has a sports bar, with pool tables, darts and dominoes; a rather quieter cocktail bar; a lounge bar with an open fire; and, best of all, a side room which has become the pictorial museum of the long-defunct Glyn Valley Tramway, its history explained in a vast number of captioned photographs. This room also houses a baby grand piano, often commandeered for an impromptu performance on Friday nights by the local choir (at other times the comfortable piano stool is likely to be commandeered by the pub cat). There is also a restaurant, well known locally for its three-course Sunday lunches, a snip at under a fiver, and for its local trout and pheasant dishes. Parties of visitors to the nearby slate mine and museum at Chwarel Wynne can take advantage of "mine, wine and dine" evenings! More prosaically, the pub also acts as a take-away fish and chip shop. There are a few tables on a patio overlooking the village playground and the wooded hills hemming in the valley. The accommodation includes a honeymoon suite with a four-poster bed. Activities locally include pony trekking, fishing on the River Ceiriog, rough shooting and walking, and in the pub itself there are regular skittles evenings and a weekly trivia quiz.

GLYNDYFRDWY
Berwyn Arms

Tel: (049 083) 210
On A5

✗ lunchtime and evening

🍴

⌂

🍺 Burtonwood Bitter

The new landlord has ambitious plans for this handsome former coaching inn, right on the A5 to the west of the village. There will be an extension to the popular Riverside Bar, a newly-constructed patio taking full advantage of the breathtaking views across the Dee valley, and a family beer garden to supplement the tables now fronting the inn. The lounge, with its intricate carvings above the bar counter and its milestone showing distances to Holyhead (71 miles), Corwen (4 miles 2 furlongs) and Llangollen (5 miles 6 furlongs) embedded in the wall, will remain largely untouched. The Riverside Bar, cosy and convivial, looks directly out onto the Dee valley, with the river flanked by the trees below and the inviting, steep green slopes of Llantysilio Mountain beyond. Fishing talk dominates, hardly surprisingly since the Berwyn Arms has the fishing rights to a two-mile stretch of the river (permits available over the bar). Residents also have the use of a further lounge dominated by an extraordinary original fireplace, while the stables of the seventeenth-century inn now form a spacious restaurant and breakfast room. Just along the road is Owain Glyndwr's Mount, the site of one of the Welsh prince's former strongholds.

GRAIANRHYD
Rose & Crown

Tel: (08243) 727
On the B5430

✗ lunchtime and evening

🍺 Marston Burton Best Bitter, Pedigree; guest beers

An isolated and — given its reputation for good food — surprisingly spartan rural pub situated at a crossroads, the Rose and Crown is split into two very distinct areas served by one long bar. The public bar area is best described as unspoilt and traditional; there are few creature comforts here, though the tiled floor, darts board and open fire create a homely atmosphere. The small and intimate low-lit lounge area, not the easiest place to order a drink during busy periods, when the counter is thickly peopled with regulars on bar stools, is popular with diners as well as local real ale drinkers. Vegetarian dishes are always available, and a far from expensive full breakfast is served between half-past eight and ten o'clock. The Marston's ales are usually in good form and are supplemented, especially at weekends, by guest beers from around the country – Ringwood's and Wadworth's have been featured in the past, and Sam Powell's Samson was recently sighted. The lounge, with a collection of mugs hanging from the ceiling, prints and maps on the roughly rendered walls, red velvet bar stools around low brass-topped tables, and bench seating in a big window alcove, is an excellent spot for an aperitif before adjourning to the separate restaurant. It can become dangerously addictive for those who simply drop in for a pint of Pedigree!

GRAIGFECHAN
Three Pigeons Inn

Tel: (08242) 3178
On the B5429 three miles south of Ruthin

✕ lunchtime and evening

◎

⊗

⊟ **Stones Best Bitter, Draught Bass**

Substantial alterations are well underway which will have the effect of transforming what was once a classic small country inn into something rather different and perhaps a little less "special". The Three Pigeons, a free house in the best tradition, is the only pub in this book to have appeared in *every* "Good Beer Guide" since 1974, but its appeal in those days was as a simple, basic local with marvellous views across the peaceful countryside of the southern Vale of Clwyd. Now, whilst a great deal of charm remains – not least the continuing tradition of fetching the ale from the cellar in big jugs and then decanting it, several pints at a time, into beer mugs – there is a clear distinction between the "old" traditional pub and the newer extension, with a growing emphasis on food. And yet – the food is excellent, with fresh home cooking on Friday and Saturday evenings, and the remote location is as tantalisingly appealing as ever. Try the after-dark approach from the south, along the desperately narrow road through Pentrecelyn; amazingly this is classified as a B road! Then sit in the plain old bar, or better still the back lounge with its heavily-jugged beamed ceiling, piano, big solid tables and door leading to the verandah and that splendid view.

GRESFORD
Griffin

Tel: (097 883) 2231
The Green (B5373)

🅱

🍺 Greenall's Mild, Bitter

A pub which manages to pack quite a lot into relatively little, the Griffin is still rather better known for its location next to one of the "Seven Wonders of Wales" than for its intrinsic merits. The wonder in question is the Gresford Bells, in the parish church just across The Green – and very cacophonous they seem to casual pubgoers who choose to visit the Griffin on a Saturday afternoon busy with wedding ceremonies. The church is one of the best parish churches in Wales, its tower rising beyond knarled eighteenth-century yew trees and its stained glass well worth seeing. The village, big and bustling though now relieved of much through traffic, stands well to the north of the site of Gresford Colliery, now reclaimed for new-style industry but still remembered for one of the twentieth-century's worst mining disasters. The Griffin has no such history, whether illustrious or macabre, but it is a very popular local with a big solid bar counter serving several different areas. There is a boisterous drinking area with darts board, a comfortable and much quieter side room complete with piano, and a strange long narrow room with a single table running the length of it. Lots of bric-a-brac decorates the walls and ceiling, and there's an enthusiastic and convivial feel to the place.

GRONANT
Gronant Inn

Tel: (07456) 3725
Llanasa Road. OS093831

✗ lunchtime

▨

◁ **Marston Mercian Mild, Burton Best Bitter**

An unassuming village pub in the middle of Gronant, a separate community in its own right but nowadays heavily dependent upon Prestatyn, the town at the bottom of the hill, the Gronant Inn is a cosy and quite old two-roomed house. From across the road it betrays its former role as two separate houses, even to the extent of still having two separate front doors. One half of the pub is whitewashed render, the other naked stone with climbing roses above the door and curling attractively around one of the windows. An unusually scenic inn sign shows a rocky stream rippling under trees; if its inspiration was local, it was not in the immediate vicinity. To one side is a safe, fenced garden with swings and a slide, while the younger generation will also be interested in the friendly horse in the field opposite the pub. Inside there are lots of solid wood tables, a few of them brass-topped, and plenty of high bar stools for gossiping villagers; in the bar darts, pool and dominoes are all popular. At the bottom of the hill is the busy A548, leading to Prestatyn in one direction and Point of Ayr colliery and Mostyn Dock in the other; more tranquil country lies to the south, with the little lanes around Llanasa and Whitford full of unsuspected interest.

GWERNYMYNYDD
Owain Glyndwr

Tel: (0352) 2913
Glyndwr Road (a mile from the A494 at Rainbow Garage)

✗ lunchtime

☺

◁ **Burtonwood Dark Mild, Bitter**

A thousand feet up in the hills to the south-west of Mold, the Owain Glyndwr has spectacular views towards and across the distant Dee estuary, and across the Cheshire Plain; it is said that you can see five counties from the front door. The setting is somewhat out of the ordinary: at the end of a row of terraced cottages a country mile from Gwernymynydd and seemingly a long way from anywhere else – though very close to America! The approach from the A494 is straightforward but requires perseverance when the pub fails to appear after the first couple of minutes. Inside there is a friendly welcome and a total lack of pretentiousness. It's a typically Welsh country pub, full of character and with its fair share of characters, some of them noted for their vocal attributes. There is one big room, with a real fire, a pool table and a rather prominent television much in demand with the local racing fraternity. A notable extra is the wide selection of wines by the bottle or half bottle for drinkers whose palates need a change from the excellent Burtonwood beers. Close by are the county town of Mold, generally dull but with an entertaining street market and the eclectic Theatr Clwyd, and of course the Clwydian range, with Foel Fenlli and its hillfort within easy reach.

HALKYN
Britannia

Tel: (0352) 780 272
Pentre Road, Halkyn Mountain
(200 yards from the A55)

✗	lunchtime and evening
🍴	
🍽	lunchtime
⛺	
🍺	**Lees GB Mild, Bitter, Moonraker (winter)**

This marvellous stone-built country pub, on a hillside above the A55 dual carriageway and with wide views across the sands of the Dee estuary to the Wirral, is extremely popular with the local farming community and justifiably attracts many tourists too. Some of the latter might have been drawn by the yellow-stone church and the castellated lodges of Halkyn Castle, though the scarred slopes of Halkyn Mountain, with its limestone quarries and old lead mines, are perhaps more intrinsically interesting. The Britannia itself is reputed to be 500 years old, although the first written evidence dates back only to the 1750s. It became a John Willie Lees house in 1947, and now has an enviable reputation for these distinctive Manchester ales, including the fearsome Moonraker barley wine served straight from the cask in winter. There are four rooms in which to enjoy the beer, with a games room catering for pool addicts; an intimate restaurant offering an adventurous selection of wholesome meals (children and vegetarians are both well catered for, incidentally); an attractive lounge bar, and – perhaps the best of the lot – a small but airy snug with photographs of celebrated Halkyn cricket teams of long ago decorating the walls. Outside there are a few seats set above a combined car park and farmyard; indeed it's not too hard to imagine that this is still a country farmhouse rather than a pub.

glasses in the Black Lion Bersham

HANMER
Hanmer Arms

Tel : (094 874) 532
*A quarter of a mile from the
A539, 6 miles west of Whitchurch*

✕ lunchtime and evening

🍴

☺

🛏

🍺 Tetley Bitter, Ind Coope
Burton Ale

This is an old country inn which has been carefully updated to form a cheerful, welcoming family-run hotel, with the bars and guest rooms set around a cobbled courtyard. The pub lies in a conservation area close to the northern end of the scenic Hanmer Mere, a tranquil lake covering some 45 acres and very much the chief attraction of Hanmer, a pleasant village in the English Maelor and formerly part of the curious entity known as "Flintshire (detached)". It is an outstanding base for walking, fishing, golfing or just exploring this fascinating borders area. The accommodation is highly regarded and whilst it certainly appeals to businessmen (conference facilities are available for the dedicated) it also includes rooms suitable for families; and a new family room is planned for the pub, widening the appeal of the place still further. The food, in the separate restaurant or the bistro-style bar, is excellent and includes as a speciality meat dishes based on local products; vegetarians are equally well provided for, however. A separate and well-equipped games room caters especially for pool and darts fans. The beer range has varied over recent years, and whilst it is still enterprising in comparison with many of the local pubs some will mourn the passing of the Marston's Pedigree (doubtless drowning their sorrows with Burton Ale?).

HAWARDEN
Blue Bell

Tel : (0244) 532995
Highway (B5125)

✕ lunchtime

🍺 Wilson's Original Bitter,
Webster's Yorkshire Bitter

Right in the middle of the historic village of Hawarden, the Blue Bell is a pub which seems to generate a tremendous community spirit, with all sorts of activities based here, including a football team, two quiz sides and a golfing society. Such is its popularity that at weekends it can become very full indeed, and since it attracts younger drinkers it can become quite boisterous too, though older drinkers are also made to feel very welcome. It is not a pub to drive to, though – negotiating the car park (the narrow entrance to which is shared with the pub next door) can be problematical at the best of times. The lounge bar is comfortable and features brasses above the fireplace and plates on a rather higher shelf, while even the bar counter itself is half-timbered. There are lots of horsey artefacts including a bulky halter, and a bevy of prints; the rustic theme is, however, slightly misplaced in a pub which has a strongly urban feel to it. The village, at the gateway to North Wales (but thankfully no longer on the A55), has a ruined castle, and there is another, rather more romantic one built by the Welsh princes at nearby Ewloe; the early Victorian "new" castle became the home of W. E. Gladstone.

LLANARMON-YN-IAL
Raven

Tel: (08243) 787
On the B5431

✗ lunchtime and evening

🍴

☺

📠

🍺 Burtonwood Dark Mild, Bitter

Opposite the double-aisled village church, its arcades supported by octagonal timber columns, and set behind a pleasant beer garden, the Raven is a picture postcard example of a village pub. The garden is an ideal place for a relaxing drink on a fine summer evening, but the bar too has its attractions after sundown, with separate drinking areas, low-beamed ceilings and (a surprise to find it still there) a brown skull tucked away in a little cupboard within the inglenook. The locals tend to congregate in the back part of the bar (the newish bar counter is no improvement here) with its darts board and spartan furnishings, while visitors are more likely to sit at the tables in the front bar, including benches under the inglenook and seats and copper-topped tables to the side of the piano. The separate lounge bar tends to act as an overflow room and is consequently not always open during the week; at weekends it functions as a dining room. The surroundings are delight-fully peaceful, with a quiet lane leading to the Clwydians (and Offa's Dyke Path for the strenu-ously inclined) and little limestone outcrops around the village hinting at the quarrying which disfigures the local landscape in places. The Yale family, emigrants who founded Yale University, took their name from "Ial" which translates as "a cultivated region". The home cooking is worth noting and the accommodation simple but adequate and inexpensive, in keeping with this excellent, unspoilt little inn.

at Llanarmon

LLANBEDR DYFFRYN CLWYD
Griffin

Tel: (08242) 2792
On the A494

✗ lunchtime and evening

🅳 Robinson Best Bitter

Llanbedr Dyffryn Clwyd lies at the foot of the Clwydians, just to the south of Moel Fammau (the mother mountain), which is crowned by the Jubilee Tower, built in 1810 to celebrate George III's golden jubilee. The turnpike road from Mold to Ruthin descended through Llanbedr to the Vale of Clwyd, and a former toll house stands to one side of the Griffin, once a coaching inn, and later used by Charles de Gaulle during the Second World War. Its comfortable bedrooms, some of them with beamed ceilings, now cater largely for tourists. The inn, with its latticed casement windows, has all the looks of an early nineteenth-century country hotel, and the big porch with climbing roses adds to its charm. To the left of the entrance there is a small, cheery public bar, while to the right is a restaurant with an extensive menu (mango with honey and yogurt a tempting starter). The lounge bar, its firebreast adorned with brasses and host to a blazing log fire in winter, appears small but opens out onto a large and rather plain room and then, quite unexpectedly, a relaxing and very well-hidden area with settees and a piano. Outside there is a small patio and an attractive garden with panoramic views of the hills.

LLANDEGLA
Crown

Tel: (097 888) 228
At A525/A5104 jct

✗ lunchtime and evening

🅳 Lees Bitter

Four hundred years ago this was a farmhouse and drovers' inn; in those days Llandegla (now a sleepy village beside the River Alun) was a centre for cattle drovers and held large and important cattle fairs. More recently the Crown became a coaching inn of some repute, largely because of its position at the junction of the roads from Wrexham to Ruthin, and Chester to Corwen. Now its main function is to provide sustenance for travellers on these roads, many of them crossing the Llandegla grouse moors on their way to the Horseshoe Pass and Llangollen, or to the Vale of Clwyd. Meals are served in the bar or the restaurant, and are of excellent quality, with home-made steak-and-kidney pie and local trout apparently amongst the favourites. The Lees Bitter, in the small and pleasantly old-fashioned public bar or the much larger lounge, is also eminently drinkable. The lounge bar, cluttered but cheerful and eye-catching, attracts a cosmopolitan crowd with its rough stone walls, toby jugs and plates, and inglenook with horse brasses. It's just as well that the pub is so convivial, set as it is high in the middle of the lonely heather moors, and miles from anywhere, though close to Offa's Dyke Path. It used to be "dry" on Sundays, and older locals can still remember making the journey to the Liver at Rhydtalog for a drink on the Sabbath.

Plough

Tel: (097 888) 672
On the A525

✗ lunchtime and evening

🛏

☒ **Robinson Best Bitter**

A large, smart roadside inn catering for travellers on the Wrexham to Ruthin road, the Plough has a large car park at the front, a beer garden to the side, and, beyond the pub's own caravan park, the wide sweep of the Llandegla moors behind, with little hills and valleys mainly clothed with heather but broken up by occasional conifer plantations. Perhaps the most notable feature of the interior, and one which immediately confronts customers, is the splendid large Welsh dresser. There is a separate restaurant to the right of the entrance, with a large but still quite intimate lounge bar area to the left. The end wall supports a highly unusual work of art — two wooden plates, one on either side of the fireplace, with an old lady knitting on the left and an old man feeding her yarn on the right. Through an arch is a separate rear lounge. Both bars have subdued lighting and comfortable seating, together with the usual collection of brasses and other artefacts. Food has a high profile in the Plough, with bar meals and an à la carte menu at lunchtime and during the evening, and there are also two letting bedrooms. Surprisingly this has only been a Robinson's tied house since the 1970s; its previous history is uncertain, though it was a farm in the days of the "goose walks", when flocks of geese, their feet tarred for the long waddle to market, were shepherded along together for protection from thieves.

LLANDULAS
Dulas Arms

Tel: (0492) 515747
Abergele Road

✗ lunchtime and evening

🛏

💷

🏠

🍺 **Lees GB Mild, Bitter**

The Dulas Arms is a surprisingly large pub providing a comprehensive range of facilities. Across the former main road it faces a huge limestone quarry, whilst the new A55 expressway roars by below and to the rear. The main lounge bar is very large but is neatly divided into a number of distinct areas, with stools at the bar for the gregarious and tables around the walls, which are adorned with a good deal of brassware together with prints and an antique map of Denbighshire. There is also, inexplicably, a large brass-bound chest on display. A pleasant snug, light and airy, leads to a fully-fledged restaurant, while a family room lies beyond a curtain and up a flight of stairs. A large beer garden with lots of play equipment overlooks the sea (but unfortunately also overlooks the expressway, and is hence subject to the incessant drone of traffic). The "Dulas special" is Brontosaurus steak (including a complimentary ticket to Dinosaur World) but there are also grills, fish dishes and a wide range of other delicacies. Sporty customers will find a darts board, neatly tucked away in an alcove beyond a model cannon, and a pool table. An outgoing sort of pub, 200 years old, rambling and full of character – and the natives are friendly too! – the Dulas Arms is highly recommended as a "halfway house" for those travelling along the A55.

Valentine

Tel: (0492) 518189
Mill Street (B5443)

✗ lunchtime and evening

🍴

☺

🍺 **M & B Mild, Draught Bass**

A shy little pub, tucked down below the level of the main road, the Valentine has been tastefully renovated and has character, history and a warm welcome. Once a home-brew house (bottles embossed with the Valentine Ales logo still exist), it later became a small hotel and is now simply a friendly village local, although it is also extremely popular with holidaymakers in summer. Neither bar is exactly roomy – indeed the public bar, cosy and warm, is spectacularly tiny – but they are full of interest. The lounge has an inviting coal and log fire and walls adorned with old prints of Llandulas, pictures of the pub itself, and a selection of landscape paintings (which are on sale to customers). There is a large mirror advertising Worthington's Pale Ales (by appointment to HRH the Prince of Wales), though he like everyone else would have to be satisfied with Draught Bass and M & B's unmemorable mild now. The beamed ceiling and subdued lighting help to create a relaxed atmosphere; and the fire ensures that this is an excellent warming winter pub too. The Valentine also has a children's room and (under an arch, and located by following the public footpath sign) a beer garden, with tables, a little lawn and the remains of an old red telephone box.

LLANFAIR TALHAIARN
Swan

Tel: (074 584) 233
Swan Square (off A548)

✗ lunchtime and evening

🍴

☺

🛏

🍺 **Marston Mercian Mild, Burton Best Bitter, Pedigree**

Tucked away from the main road through the Elwy valley, the Swan is a real centre of village life and an outstanding example of an unspoilt traditional village inn, with no frills but with well-kept beer, substantial bar meals and simple but good value accommodation. It has, in fact, exactly the kind of all-round appeal which today's pub designers, straightjacketed in their modish, segmented concepts, couldn't create in a hundred years. There's a welcome for all, with kids particularly well catered for in a pleasant family room which opens onto the pub's secluded garden. The vibrant heart of the Swan, though, and the place to make for in order to soak up the atmosphere, is the front bar, plain and unfussy but exuding warmth and hospitality. Marston's are to be commended just for leaving it alone! The village is the natural centre of the unspoilt and indeed largely unknown Elwy valley and is probably best known to fishermen; the view of bridge, river and hillside village is a classic of its kind. The unique village name derives from the bard Talhaiarn, who is buried in the churchyard; the church belfry, on the other hand, is notable for its weatherfish!

Roy – the finest
Pool player in
North Wales

LLANFWROG
Cross Keys

Tel: (08242) 5281
On the B5105

✘ lunchtime and evening

🍴

🍺 **Banks Mild, Bitter**

An award-winner! The Denbighshire Free Press pub of the year for 1989, no less, the Cross Keys stands opposite the solid parish church of Llanfwrog, now effectively the western suburb of Ruthin. The church, with its squat medieval tower, the whitewashed pub and the terraced half-timbered cottages make an attractive picture. The pub stands above the road and is reached up a flight of stone steps; a few tables on an impromptu terrace cater for summer drinkers (as does the beer garden and play area at the back of the pub). The interior is unspoilt if a little cramped at busy times, and has a small bar counter, with hunting scenes above, serving a variety of rooms. The lounge, to the left of the entrance, has a nice fireplace and a lovely dark wood Welsh dresser with an impressive display of china – though it's a shame that the one-armed bandit crowds right up against it. Beyond the dresser is the dining room, boasting an extensive menu including excellent simple dishes such as savoury prawn pancake. Upstairs is a room devoted to pool and darts, and the entrance to the garden. The Banks's beer is a welcome addition to choice in the Ruthin area; years ago "real" Border bitter was the order of the day.

LLANGOLLEN
Cambrian Hotel

Tel: (0978) 860686
Berwyn Street (A5)

✘ evening

⌖

🛏

🍺 **Younger Scotch**

A weatherbeaten but unchanging hotel on the main A5 – often choked with traffic to and from Snowdonia and Holyhead – the Cambrian attracts customers with its big black and white sign high on its grey-rendered wall. Its facade is attractive, with balconied first floor windows and hanging baskets below, but inside it is down-to-earth and old-fashioned, especially in the excellent small bar. Popular with the locals, and particularly with dominoes enthusiasts, the bar has a unique atmosphere, good-humoured and tolerant, with lots of character on both sides of the bar. Children are welcome in the much quieter front lounge, and there is also a separate dining room. Close by is the busy heart of Llangollen, a tourist trap virtually throughout the year, with the wide River Dee running below the limestone cliffs of Eglwyseg, the Llangollen steam railway and the canal designed by Telford, and excellent short walks to the hilltop ruins of Castell Dinas Bran and to Plas Newydd, the home of the Ladies of Llangollen and virtually a museum of wood carvings from around Europe. A little further away are the secluded ruins of Valle Crucis, a Cistercian abbey founded in 1201.

Wynnstay Arms

Tel: (0978) 860710
Bridge Street

✕ lunchtime and evening

🍽

◎

▰

🍺 **Tetley Bitter, Ind Coope Burton Ale**

Easily overlooked in this busy town with its voracious appetite for tourists' money, the Wynnstay is a fine traditional inn, friendly and welcoming and with a variety of rooms to suit all tastes; the bed and breakfast terms are very competitive, too. The entrance passage leads directly to the back lounge, a marvellously relaxed place for a drink, all dark wood and subdued lighting, with tables and comfortable chairs around a big old fireplace and in secluded little spots around the walls. To one side of the fireplace a narrow passageway leads through to an intimate little restaurant. The front bar, reached by a rather tortuous route, is worth the trouble: an excellent example of a country town hotel bar, it is gloriously unspoilt, boasting a splendid bar counter and scrubbed wood floors. Tradition oozes out of the walls, and indeed the whole of this popular pub is furnished wholly in keeping with its seventeenth-century origins and later history. There is a separate games room for those whose need for recreation takes precedence over historical tours, together with a garden at the rear of the pub. At the bottom of Bridge Street is the River Dee, with the revitalised trackbed of the steam railway just across the bridge and Castell Dinas Bran overlooking the whole scene.

LLANSANNAN
Red Lion

Tel: (074 577) 256
On the A544

✖ lunchtime and evening

▣

⋈

⛃ Lees GB Mild, Bitter

This is a marvellous little country inn, cosy and welcoming and with a very considerable history behind it. The pub dates from the fourteenth century and although it has doubtless changed considerably since its earliest days it retains a number of quaint old features including an outstanding fireplace with settles and benches set round it, and an antique wishing-chair. It is a great venue for a quiet drink by the old-fashioned bar or for those wanting to try their hand at traditional pub games. The Red Lion functions very much as a community centre, too, and lots of locals are in evidence in the cosy back bar. Not surprisingly there are quite a few tourists who stay here, taking advantage of the very reasonably priced letting bedrooms and the substantial traditional breakfasts, and either soaking up the charm of the unspoilt Aled valley right on the doorstep or venturing further afield, to Denbigh, with its splendid castle dominating the town and overlooking the glorious long green ridge of the Clwydian Hills, or to Abergele and the seaside resorts of the Clwyd coast. Llanrwst and Snowdonia, particularly the long, forbidding ridge of the Carneddau, are also very accessible.

LLAN-Y-PWLL
Gredington
Arms

Tel: (0978) 661728
On the A534

✖ lunchtime and evening

⛃ Hydes Bitter

Although it would be damning the Gredington Arms with faint praise to refer to it as the best of a bad lot, it has to be said that the competition from other pubs in the area to the north-east of Wrexham is not overwhelming. Nevertheless the Gredington itself, unassuming though it may be, is actually a very pleasant spot for a quiet drink, and it has a separate restaurant area too. A main road pub, red-brick but with virginia creeper around the door, it is only three miles from the centre of Wrexham, on the road to Holt and (eventually) Nantwich, yet it has a remarkably rural aspect, with cows grazing peacefully in the sloping field opposite. Over the hill, however, is the impressively large Wrexham Industrial Estate. Travellers from the Wrexham direction are likely to be shocked when they step inside, for the pub is surprisingly big compared with its narrow aspect from the west. The inn sign, on the other hand, will impress everyone with its complicated coat of arms and motto. The single lounge bar is high-ceilinged, roomy and well-lit, with prints, brasses and a big tapestry providing decorative interest. There are plenty of dried flowers too. The bar menu offers relatively standard fare but the party menus are a good deal more adventurous; it's worth clubbing together to visit this one!

The Raven, at Llanarmon

LLOC
Rock

Tel: (035 271) 0049
At the A5026/A5151 jct

✗ lunchtime and evening

🍴

◎

🍺 **Burtonwood Dark Mild, Bitter**

An outstanding wayside inn, once on the main A55 (now vastly improved and moved a mile or so to the south), the Rock at Lloc still offers sustenance to travellers and to a surprising number of locals – so much so that it is often *very* busy. It's a favourite stopping point for those on the way to or from the North Wales coast. The main bar, to the right of the entrance, is small but much favoured by the locals; the juke box can be distracting but the horseracing prints are entertaining. A rather quieter adjoining area, obviously once a separate room, has rural scenes in "stained" glass in the windows and old beer bottles suspended from the ceiling. But the favourite for many drinkers here is the back lounge, reached through an archway and forming a wonderfully cosy room, full of interest. There's a neo-medieval frieze above the fireplace, a well-populated fish tank, cigarette cards displayed on the wall, an extensive collection of teapots dangling from the beamed ceilings – and a bank of four handpumps on the bar. The Lloc also offers a separate restaurant and a beer garden with a children's play area containing climbing frames and a see-saw. Highly recommended!

LOGGERHEADS
We Three
Loggerheads

Tel: (035 285) 337
On the A494

✗ lunchtime and evening

🍴

🍺 **Draught Bass**

An old pub (a list of landlords since the 1750s hangs in the lounge) but one which has been very thoroughly modernised, the Loggerheads has a good-sized bar area with the inevitable pool table, a tiny lounge with beams, horse brasses and a collection of old bottles, and, up a wide flight of stairs flanked with potted plants and even small trees, a very extensive and attractive area that has a heavy emphasis on food. Much of the attraction stems from the decoration, with lots of light wood fencing off intimate corners, ornithological prints on the walls and a selection of farm implements overhead. And if the clatter of knives and forks proves too much, drinkers can escape back down the stairs, perhaps pausing to look at the painting hanging over the stairwell. This shows two argumentative souls – at loggerheads! – and was painted by Richard Wilson, a founder member of the Royal Academy and regarded as the Father of English landscape painting, whilst he was staying at nearby Colomendy. (The third "loggerhead" referred to in the inn's title is the person viewing the painting.) Across the road is the source of much of the pub's summer custom, the Loggerheads country park, on the site of the Crosville Motor Company's Tea Gardens but now complete with interpretation centre, restored water mill, woodland walks and nature trails running beneath sheer limestone cliffs. Families from the country park are often to be spotted taking advantage of the pub's notably large patio.

MARCHWIEL
Red Lion

Tel: (0978) 262317
At the A525/A528 jct

✗ lunchtime and evening

⊲ **Marston Border Mild, Border Bitter, Pedigree**

Marchwiel has somehow clung on to its separate identity as a pleasant if rather dull village despite the clutching tentacles of Wrexham at the parish boundary; for how long is perhaps another matter. The church is perhaps best remembered for the memorial, 1767 vintage, to Simon Yorke Esqr of Erthig, "a pious temperate sensible country gentleman". His country house, Erddig, late seventeenth century in origin and more recently threatened by subsidence resulting from coalmining, is now in the hands of the National Trust and is a major attraction, not least for its splendid formal garden. Less temperate, though possibly no less sensible souls than Simon Yorke Esqr will follow their visit to Erddig with one to the Red Lion, a thriving village pub with a big, smoky and well-used public bar including a games room beyond wooden railings (note the creaking trophy cabinet) and a comfortable lounge with a low beamed ceiling plus a number of well-designed partitions to screen off little separate drinking areas. There are the obligatory prints on the walls, but also some sizeable paintings; assorted bric-a-brac, but also a yard of ale and potted plants. For the children there's lots to do in the good-sized garden, complete with playground and goldfish pond; in addition there are surprisingly rural views across open farmland towards the distant Dee valley.

MELIDEN
Red Lion

Tel: (07456) 2565
Off the A547

✕ lunchtime and evening

🍴

🍺 **Stones Best Bitter, Draught Bass, M & B Mild**

The Red Lion, next to the parish church of St Melyd and only yards from the main road to Prestatyn, was built around 1760 and began life as a grain house. One of only three survivors from the nine pubs which served the old lead mining community of Meliden a century ago, it is an attractive pub, its thick stone whitewashed walls rather oddly half-timbered, facing out towards the long ridge of the Clwydians, with lots of woodland walks nearby, many of them on National Trust land. The lounge bar has a fascinating collection of interesting and authentic weapons from the Civil War and later skirmishes, and there is also a solid, lived-in public bar. Home cooking features strongly on the menu, but the beers – which reputedly featured Higson's of Liverpool not so long ago – are now all from the Bass group. The family beer garden is large and full of interest, with a play area including slide and climbing frame, umbrella-shaded tables among the trees, and even aviaries. Fairy lights extend its attraction in the evenings, and a large sheltered area takes care of bad weather. An inscribed stone of Roman origin was unearthed in the garden recently, tempting the thought that there could have been a tavern here in Roman times – though it wouldn't have had Draught Bass!

MINERA
City Arms

Tel: (0978) 758890
Wern Road (B5426) OS275512

✖ lunchtime and evening

🍴

☺

🍺 **Ind Coope Burton Ale; Tetley Bitter**

The tradition of pubs brewing their own beer, threatened with extinction in the 1960s, has enjoyed quite a revival in recent years and scores of pubs now do so, with mixed results for beer drinkers but with some spectacularly good brews having been born. For a few years the City Arms was one of this happy breed, brewing its beers on the premises, but sadly Minera Brewery Ales are no more: the parent company, itself just a small part of Allied Breweries, put the little brewery to the sword in February 1989. The ales are sorely missed, not just by the regulars but by the many visitors who travelled here specially to try them (and will not travel here any more – presumably to the ultimate detriment of Allied Breweries). But the City Arms deserves better. It is a good family pub, situated in the lee of Minera mountain and close to the World's End beauty spot. There is an extensive children's play area, complementing the well-supported public bar, lounge with an impressive collection of over a hundred toby jugs, and separate restaurant. The bar meals, and especially the home-made steak pies, are worthy of note; vegetarian dishes are included on the menu, and the children's portions represent good value.

MOSS
Bird in Hand

Tel: (0978) 755809
Off the B5101. OS304538

✖ lunchtime

🍴

☺

🍺 **Hydes Bitter**

Fiendishly difficult to find, the Bird in Hand is an unusual pub in many ways. It lurks at the end of a dirt track road in the baffling territory of the Wrexham urban villages, very close to, but a switchback ride away from the Black Lion at Brymbo. Friendly and welcoming, it's another of the inexplicable clutch of Hydes' pubs in the immediate vicinity of Wrexham, though many of the customers who travel here come for the food just as much as the beer. The interior of the pub has a single lounge bar virtually surrounded by a whole series of rooms decorated with highly informative photographs of the local history of the area, in addition to a collection of toby jugs. The style is relaxed and pleasant, in the usual unostentatious but perfectly comfortable Hydes idiom, and there can be few better places to which those marooned in Wrexham can escape. Families are welcome in the front dining area, and there is also a garden with children's play area. From here the views, not at all as industrial as might be expected, are really spectacular. Close by is the Moss Valley country park, another indication of the greening which has done so much to improve the area.

MOSTYN
Lletty Hotel

Tel: (074 556) 0292
Coast Road (A548)

✗ lunchtime

⋈

⊲ **Burtonwood Dark Mild, Bitter**

A curious and characterful pub of quite some historical interest, the Lletty is tucked into the hillside at a bend in the main coast road near Mostyn Dock, originally a coal port, its cargo mostly bound for Ireland but now, judging from recent sightings, mostly concerned with timber. The Liverpool ferry ran from here until the 1890s. The Lletty's customers include dockers, and it was previously the haunt of coalminers too. But the pub's history goes back much further, to 1699. It was formerly a posting house and it has also catered in its time for smugglers plying the Dee shoreline. Above the doorway is inscribed "The Honeft Man", and there is also a gaudy figure of the honest man himself – an early landlord of the pub who went bankrupt in his alternative occupation as a sheep butcher yet returned in order to repay his creditors. Now the Lletty, somewhat refurbished a few years ago and quite attractive externally, whitewashed with highlights picked out in green and with flower tubs along the frontage, is a useful stopping point for Merseysiders halfway to the North Wales coast. It's a pub with one big bar, honest, unpretentious and brassy, and with interesting stained glass above the bar counter. All in all it's worth a detour, as is the bizarre nineteenth-century folly of Drybridge Lodge on top of a tunnel in the road to Whitford.

OLD COLWYN
Plough

Tel: (0492) 515387
282 Abergele Road

✗ lunchtime and evening

🍴

🍺 Greenall's Mild, Bitter,
Thomas Greenall's Original

Outstandingly refurbished to create an excellent, comfortable drinking environment with a warm and welcoming atmosphere, the Plough has outgrown its old days as a posting house (though the former stables remain at the back of the pub) but remains excellent value for a visit. It is especially useful for those staying in Colwyn Bay and looking for a decent pint in a good pub atmosphere. Lots of use has been made of dark wood, though this sober atmosphere is lightened by the prints around the walls. There is a big black fireplace with an old range and much ancillary brassware, and old ploughs and other agricultural implements dangle from the ceiling. Good lunches are served in the bar and in the neatly partitioned restaurant, itself nicely furnished and with heavy drapes; the menu caters for children and vegetarians. The beer is lovingly cared for and includes the relatively new Thomas Greenall's Original, well worth sampling here. At one side is a small garden area; perhaps the most notable exterior feature, however, is the inn sign, boldly proclaiming Yr Aradr to travellers in one direction (to the possible confusion of the monoglot English!) and the Plough to those heading the other way.

PENLEY
Dymock Arms

Tel: (094 874) 221
On the A539

✗ lunchtime and evening

⌾

🍺 Marston Burton Best Bitter, Pedigree

The Dymock Arms is a real find, an excellent free house in a parish right on the English border, with the lake country around Ellesmere in Shropshire only a few minutes' drive away. The building itself, alongside the A539 Ruabon to Whitchurch road, is splendidly evocative and is reputedly of fifteenth-century origin. There are three public rooms, though connoisseurs will probably by-pass the bar and the dining room, with its vegetarian delights prominent in an extensive menu, and make for the superb 400 year-old snug. It is a privilege to be able to drink in this wonderfully maintained little bar, which is one of the finest remaining examples of its kind. Inside the snug, incidentally, is an original black kitchen range manufactured in 1888 by the Birdsall Bros of Whitchurch, eight miles to the east. Families, deprived of the pleasures of the snug, will be cheered by the news that there is a garden with a play area outside, while Latin scholars need hardly be reminded that the pub's motto – *Pro rege et lege dimico* – translates as "diligent for the Queen and law". Local sights likely to tempt the curious include the moated site of Penley Hall, the half-timbered Tudor Court, and the thatched, early nineteenth-century Madras primary school.

PEN-Y-MYNYDD
White Lion

Tel: (0244) 543204
Chester Road (A5118)

🍺 Marston Border Bitter

An absolute must for lovers of the traditional pub, the White Lion has remained virtually unchanged for decades. Lovingly run by three sisters, one of whom has seen more than seventy years there, it offers little in the way of creature comforts but has a wonderful homeliness and operates almost as a community centre, with all the regular customers (and some of the not-so-regular) known by name. The best evenings in this extraordinary place are akin to a family reunion. The beer is excellent and as cheap as any in the neighbourhood, and the money disappears into an old-fashioned till. The front room is the place for gentle conversation; a snug to the side of the bar itself caters for those wanting a little more privacy. There are no frills here but the White Lion should be seen and enjoyed by every drinker sated by a diet of "theme" pubs and identikit bars; it really is an amazing pub, a perfect example of the kind of basic boozer which you were convinced had disappeared years ago. But be warned – the opening hours are restricted, and those hoping for a drink in the early evening are likely to be condemned to a long wait in the car park.

Cyclist hitting a glass of
Burtonwood in the Raven
at Llanarmon

PONTFADOG
Graig

Tel: (069 172) 712
Off the B4500. OS234379

✗ lunchtime and evening

🕯

◎

🍺 **Marston Pedigree**

The special feature of this friendly if relatively basic free house is its marvellous location, perched high above the River Ceiriog and with lovely views across the valley to the wooded slopes of the declining Berwyn Mountain ridge. The intrepid will drive up to the pub, via a steep and twisting lane, with inevitable problems if they meet another car halfway. Others will leave their car on the main Ceiriog valley road, cross the river, foaming in its rocky bed, and approach the Graig by footpath. The path slants steeply up the river cliff, snakes round the back of the pub (a little clearing up would not go amiss here) and reaches the terrace and the view. Inside this compact little pub there is not a great deal of room, though it's cosily and efficiently arranged and there is also a separate pool room. The Graig is a favourite halting place for the pony trekkers who are thick on the ground around here. Not least of the attractions for them, and for walkers and others exploring this quiet side valley, is the full range of bar meals, together with an excellent pint of Pedigree, the replacement for the Lees bitter which used to be sold here in days gone by.

RHEWL
Sun Inn

Tel: (0978) 861043
Two miles from the A5

✗ lunchtime and evening

🕯

◎

🍺 **Felinfoel Bitter**

The royal road to the Sun starts in Glyndyfrdwy – but not after a session in the Berwyn Arms, for this road takes a lot of concentration, running picturesquely alongside the Dee one minute, climbing sharply onto the flanks of Llantysilio Mountain for terrific views along the valley and across the hills hemming it in, then dipping back down to the river and, eventually, the little hamlet of Rhewl. The Sun traces its history back to the fourteenth century, when it was a drover's inn, and one envies the cattlemen their unhurried journey through this outstanding landscape, and their pint at such a delightful inn. Even they would not have been drinking Felinfoel bitter, though; it is typically idiosyncratic that the real ale here should be, uniquely for Clwyd, from far-off Llanelli. The tiny, white-painted pub, with its uneven roof-line, climbing roses around the porch, stone-flagged floors and real settles, attracts walkers, cyclists and more vicarious tourists by the drove (no pun intended) in summer, and has a welcome for all, with a beer garden, games room and good, filling bar food. Curiously, the bar features coalmining mementoes on the wall. A great pub in an idyllic setting: do try it (using the easier road from near Llangollen if you must!).

RHOSESMOR
Red Lion

Tel: (0352) 780570
Village Road (B5123). OS213681

✗ lunchtime

🍺 **Burtonwood Dark Mild, Bitter**

The Red Lion, a compact inn situated off the beaten track on the road from Mold to Holywell, is an unexpected gem. Whilst it has to be admitted that the immediate surroundings are not all that attractive, the *cognoscenti* are far from deterred and often the two small bars are packed. Both bars are low-ceilinged and boast roaring fires in winter; both are very popular with the locals, who can choose between the slightly spartan public bar with its scrubbed floors and little tables, or the rather more comfortable lounge. The pub is a listed building and is known to have been existence in 1703. Originally it was known as the Black Lion and the licensee at that time was a Reverend Williams. Now the Red Lion offers a superb welcome, a fine pint, a varied selection of excellent bar food and even the chance to take part in a friendly quiz most evenings (though the local quiz league team takes some beating!). And on Saturday evening there is Welsh singing, perhaps as a warm-up for chapel the next morning. After a session here a stroll to the Iron Age fort close by at Moel-y-Gaer, with its spectacular views to the Clwydians and the Dee estuary, might well be called for.

RHYDTALOG
Liver Inn

Tel: (082 43) 244
On the A5104

✗ lunchtime and evening

🍺

☺

🍺 Hydes Bitter

The focus of the tiny settlement of Rhydtalog – a mere nine houses located "between the four bridges", one on each road leading from the crossroads at which the pub stands – the Liver is a squat old building, yet another former coaching inn (what used to be the stable block is now the restaurant), on the edge of Llandegla moor. The entrance porch leads into a cosy bar area with mellow stuccoed walls and an open coal fire; the lounge area has an impressive collection of Britannia tables and piped background music. There is also a children's room and a separate restaurant with an adjacent dance floor, also used as function room. The restaurant is open for lunches and evening meals in summer (and, if booked, in winter too) and there is bar food throughout the day. The car park is the site of Sunday morning car boot sales fortnightly in winter, and the pub also hosts the weekly meetings of the Milestone Motor Club and many other functions; essentially, though, it is a quiet country pub meeting the needs of travellers along the Chester to Corwen road. It is also the start (or end) of a notable pub crawl taking in the Lees and Robinson's pubs in Llandegla, the Raven at Llanarmon-yn-Ial for Burtonwood, and the Rose and Crown at Graianrhyd, with its guest beers: but take a sober driver.

RHYL
Galley

Tel: (0745) 353432
Vale Road (A525)

🍺

🍺 Marston Mercian Mild, Burton Best Bitter

A very popular drinkers' pub on the outskirts of this bustling Victorian resort town at the mouth of the River Clwyd, the Galley is classically suburban in style, big, high and bulky, painted maroon-and-white and with a fairly extraordinary ship on its colourful innsign. There's a guarantee of excellent real ale from a landlord who has been a publican locally for some 30 years. The bar, plain and quite sparsely decorated, is small and caters mainly for the locals, while the lounge, extended not so long ago and formed by the opening out of what were previously separate small rooms, has a few nautical artefacts including a ship's wheel and a comfortable and quite private area at the back. Previously known as the Queen's Arms, the pub has been a landmark on the Denbigh road for years and it is a port of call for many escaping either from the miles of holiday camps along the shoreline or from the rather brasher forms of amusement available nearer the sea. Amongst the other attractions nearby are the castle ruins at Rhuddlan (the scene of bitter Anglo-Welsh struggles from the Battle of Rhuddlan in 796 until Edward I built the castle and planned town in 1278), the waterfalls at Dyserth and the cathedral city of St Asaph.

Millbank

Tel: (0745) 342885
Grange Road

✗ lunchtime and evening

◎

🍺 **Tetley Bitter, Ind Coope Burton Ale**

The present Millbank Inn, an Ansells (and thus Allied Breweries) house lost in suburbia but actually not that far from the centre of Rhyl, was built in 1937 right next to the original Millbank, a former beerhouse (licensed to sell beer only) which is still standing but is now a private house. A photograph of the former pub in its heyday is displayed in its successor, and it is worth looking at this and then wandering outside to see the tiny, white-painted building in the flesh so to speak. The new Millbank is in many ways a typical inter-war roadhouse – it could have been plucked from Ansells' West Midlands heartland – though it had the good fortune to be completed before the Second World War, and thus to escape the austerity measures introduced into pub-building immediately afterwards. It is, therefore, interesting both externally, with fake half-timbering a feature of the high gable-end, and inside, where there is a richly wood-panelled lounge. There is also a bar, featuring pub games, and a children's room, while one old-fashioned window advertises in etched glass the "outdoor department". Popular and friendly, the Millbank has a fine pint of Burton Ale and is undoubtedly worth the trek from the town centre.

RUABON
Duke of
Wellington

Tel: (0978) 820381
50 yards from High Street
(B5606)

✗ lunchtime and evening

🍴

🍺 **Marston Border Mild,**
Pedigree

An odd place for beer drinkers, Ruabon. There are plenty of pubs, with a reasonable choice, but none of them seems outstanding. Perhaps the most interesting is the Great Western, a Burton-wood house which brewed its own beer until 1937 and which evokes memories of Ruabon's days as a major interchange for steam trains; but the future of the pub is uncertain. One of the most welcoming and comfortable is the Duke of Wellington, an old Border Breweries house in a well-pubbed area just below Ruabon's gaunt parish church and adjacent little round-house, formerly used as a lock-up for prisoners on their way from Chester to Shrewsbury gaol. The "Duke", down in a hollow below the main road and approached via a narrow walled lane, features a bright and often busy bar, very traditional in style, and a lounge which has been rather well modernised to form a quiet and relaxing atmosphere – with the Duke of Wellington himself looking down on the proceedings. A good choice of bar meals is available here, too. A word of warning for bitter drinkers, though: the Pedigree is excellent but the "ordinary" bitter is, regrettably, a keg beer served through a false handpump.

RUTHIN
Wine Vaults

Tel: (082 42) 2067
St Peter's Square

🛏

💷

🍺 **Robinson Best Bitter, Old Tom (winter)**

A small town-centre hotel with two friendly and pleasant bars, the Wine Vaults has one priceless asset which comes into its own on fine summer days – the verandah under the pillared upper storeys, provided with a few simple benches and tables and possessing a superb view of activity in St Peter's Square, the heart of this lively, attractive market town. The pub's other special attraction is, however, a bonus for residents

Wine Vaults, Ruthin

only: it has both bowling green and tennis courts reserved for their use. The lounge bar, dazzling its customers with some rather garish lighting behind the big curving bar counter, has lots of tall bar stools much favoured by the locals, some nice wildlife prints on the walls, and copper pans and other such items hanging from the ceiling. A side room is dominated by a centrally-situated pool table. The Wine Vaults dates from 1480 and contributes to the historical interest of the town centre. It stands opposite the marvellous old Lordship Courthouse and prison, dating from the early fifteenth-century but now a bank, and Maen Huail, a rough block of limestone of legendary interest, outside another nicely half-timbered bank, is just down the street. George Borrow, visiting Ruthin in 1854, chose to stay elsewhere (where the duck was "capital"); he found Ruthin "a dull town" but consoled himself by wandering where Owain Glyndwr had sacked and fired the town in 1400, thereby signalling the start of the "Welsh insurrection".

ST ASAPH
Swan

Tel: (0745) 582284
The Roe (A525)

⊗

🍺 Marston Border Mild, Burton Best Bitter, Pedigree

Aptly described in a recent edition of the "Good Beer Guide" as "the locals' local", the Swan gets a narrow vote over a number of other worthy pubs in this unexpectedly ordinary cathedral city. It is worth shopping around though – try the **New Inn**, for example, with its Lees beers, and the **Bull**, a quaint little Marston's pub on Lower Street. The Swan, also tied to Marston, has excellent beer and a really warm welcome for all; plain and unpretentious it may be, but it certainly has an engaging atmosphere. There is only one bar – though the windows promise a lounge, smoke room and taproom! – but it serves a varied clientele, from those dropping in for a quick pint to those intent on a game of darts, dominoes or pool. There's plenty of bench-style seating, and visual interest is provided, *inter alia*, by the old mirrors on the walls. The Swan is pretty difficult to miss for those coming off the A55 and into St Asaph from the north-west: the vivid mustard colour-washing is fairly noticeable, the windows are picked out in black, and a pro-fusion of flowers and outsize butterflies add colour to the front elevation. For cathedral buffs St Asaph's rather small, homely version with its squat fourteenth-century tower is only a stroll away.

WREXHAM
Horse & Jockey

Tel: (0978) 351081
Hope Street

✗ lunchtime

🍺 **Tetley Bitter**

The Horse and Jockey, convivial and popular, is an historic thatched pub which has somehow managed to survive in the middle of the decidedly less historic town of Wrexham. Right in the middle of Wrexham's shopping centre, and close to the Central station, the building has had an eventful but by no means unusual history. It originated as a pair of cottages and became a beerhouse known as the Colliers in 1840. Twenty-eight years later it was transformed into the Horse and Jockey; later it became one of the few tied houses of Bierne's Albion Brewery on Tower Hill, and when that brewery closed down in 1938 it was received into its present ownership, now part of the giant Allied Breweries. Both the lounge and the public bar have a good deal of bare brickwork and exposed beams, and the atmosphere of the place strikes the right balance between cheerful modernity and respect for tradition. The inn sign displayed in the lounge depicts the legendary jockey Fred Archer, who died in 1886 at the age of 29. Contemporary drinkers with an interest in the turf congregate here, too, following the sport on the big television in the public bar.

Nag's Head

Tel: (0978) 261177
Mount Street

✕ lunchtime

🍺 Marston Border Bitter,
Pedigree, Merrie Monk, Owd
Rodger (winter)

Once the showpiece pub of the former Border Breweries combine, the Nag's Head is an ancient and attractive building with leaded windows. The old brewery, now sadly underused, is right next door; this "Brewery tap" was the ideal spot to sample the beers in perfect condition. Reputedly built in 1661, the pub was subsequently rebuilt in 1941 and 1977, and it now houses a big traditional public bar with television, fruit machines and the like, yet another pool room, and a comfortable and tastefully decorated lounge which successfully contrives an "old world" atmosphere. The lunchtime food, popular with nearby workers, is unadventurous but wholesome and certainly filling. The beers may now be brewed in faraway Burton-on-Trent but there is a wide range available, especially in winter when drinkers in need of some central heating can choose between Merrie Monk, one of the strongest mild ales in the country, and the potent Owd Rodger, a classic dark barley wine. Towards the town centre is the parish church, its prosperous air reflecting Wrexham's market town wealth in medieval times, before its industrial transformation in the age of coal and iron. Worth seeing, too, is the Jacobean-style market hall, dating from 1848.

YSCEIFIOG
Fox

Tel: (0352) 720241
A mile from the A541

🍺 Banks Mild, Bitter

The Fox is an absolute gem, a classic for devotees of that most evocative of British institutions, the no-nonsense traditional pub. Unchanged for years (and in the hands of new owners who, thankfully, intend to preserve it as it is), the Fox is unspoilt by modern distractions such as juke boxes, pool tables or one-armed bandits. The staple diet here is good beer – once Greenall's, now excellent Banks's – and traditional pub games. And this commendable policy pays dividends, with locals (many of them farmers or farm workers) and the more discerning visitors crowding in to the tiny bar, many of them intent on nothing more than a pint and a game of dominoes. There is also a darts room and a traditional, unfussy lounge with a relaxed atmosphere, at its best on Friday nights when the pianist conducts the assembled company in Welsh singing. A wonderful pub with a genuine welcome for all, the Fox is well worth the short detour from the main Mold to Denbigh road, though lunchtime or early evening drinkers should check in advance to see whether the pub is likely to be open. The alternative may be to explore the seldom-used lanes and the delightfully unspoilt countryside in the immediate vicinity before trying the pub door again later!

A corner of the
Wine Vaults, Ruthin

ABERDOVEY
Penhelig Arms

Tel: (065 472) 215
On the A493

✖ lunchtime and evening

⋈

🍺 **Banks Mild Ale, Bitter**

The archetypal small seaside town hotel, the Penhelig has eleven bedrooms (nine with that all-important sea view), an excellent restaurant and a self-contained and rather stylish public bar with good traditional ale. Largely dating from the early nineteenth century, though with later accretions, the hotel was originally known as Y Dafarn Fach (the little inn). During its early days Charles Dickens was a notable visitor here. Now it is a substantial three-storey white-painted building with a balcony running above the hotel, restaurant and bar entrances. Just to the right is Penhelig Halt on the Cambrian Coast railway, while across the road is a delightful view of the Dyfi estuary, with little boats swaying on the tide, and the sand dunes near Borth in the background. The heart of the matter for beer drinkers nowadays is the Fisherman's Bar, elegantly wood-panelled and with a central fireplace, and serving interesting bar snacks. The restaurant is open for lunches and dinners seven days a week and has plenty of fish on the menu, including local sea bass, together with spinach and smoked haddock tart and duck breast sauteed pink. Nearby attractions include the Tal-y-Llyn narrow gauge railway, the harbour, jetty and beach, and for golfers a notable links course where Penhelig residents qualify for reduced green fees.

ABERSOCH
St Tudwal's
Hotel

Tel: (075 881) 2539
Main Street

✖ lunchtime and evening

🛏

⋈

🍺 **Robinson Best Mild, Best Bitter, Old Tom**

Abersoch, one of the most attractive villages on the Lleyn peninsula, has an enviably sheltered east-facing position, with magnificent views across the northern reaches of Cardigan Bay to the majestic if somewhat distant peaks of Snowdonia. The harbour, whilst it still caters for sea fishing, is heavily populated by yachting types, though visitors can also take advantage of water skiing and trips to the islands in St Tudwal's Bay, named after a sixth-century missionary. The St Tudwal's Hotel, like much of the centre of Abersoch, dates from late Victorian or Edwardian times, when the village was finding its place in tourist itineraries. White-painted and with projecting bay windows and notably solid, stumpy stone buttresses, it is a very friendly pub with widely-praised accommodation and good meals, whether in the bar or in the separate dining room. Seafood is in some demand here, including the lobsters which can sometimes be seen being brought ashore in the harbour. The lounge is smart but relaxed, an ideal spot to unwind after an arduous day on one of the excellent beaches nearby. The pub understandably attracts a strong local following as well as the shoals of summer visitors who can occasionally make the pub appear uncomfortably full at the height of the season.

BALA
White Lion Royal Hotel

Tel: (0678) 520314
66 High Street (A494)

✗ lunchtime and evening

🏵

🍴

🍺 Theakston Best Bitter, Younger No. 3

Making the most of its position right in the middle of Bala, the White Lion Royal dominates the High Street with its extravagant black-and-white half-timbering and variety of rooflines. Bold red lettering and a couple of white lions on the front elevation combine to make the hotel utterly unmistakable. Reputedly one of Wales's oldest coaching inns, and "royal" as a result of a visit from Queen Victoria, it has 26 excellent bedrooms and makes a very good touring centre for Snowdonia, the Welsh lakes (the view down Llyn Tegid, or Bala Lake, to the Aran mountains takes some beating) and the North Wales coast. The lounge bar is delightful and full of interest, with a heavily beamed ceiling, a magnificent open fireplace, a selection of high-backed wooden settles, carver chairs and little stools, and subdued lighting ideal for a quiet evening out. Copper pots decorate the shelves and window sills, while a monster fish (the legendary "gwyniad" unique to Bala Lake?) stares down from a cabinet on one wall, and another stars as part of the dramatic frieze enlivening the bar counter. There is also the smaller Poacher's Bar, and a few tables outside, perhaps too close to the traffic edging along the congested High Street to appeal to everyone. Traditional Welsh cooking is the theme for the bar meals, and there is a separate restaurant. The beer comes from Scottish & Newcastle, but at least it includes Younger No. 3, offering an interesting and unusual flavour.

BANGOR
Union Hotel

Tel : (0248) 2462
Garth Road

✗ lunchtime

🍴

◎

🛏

🍺 **Burtonwood Bitter**

Right by the water, with plenty of nautical activities visible from the windows, the Union is an unchanging locals' pub full of bric-a-brac, including a china cabinet bursting at the seams, a large collection of plates, brass kettles, a ship's wheel, and sundry candlesticks. Several different rooms open off a central servery, itself much favoured by those who prefer to drink and gossip standing up. The servery ceiling gives an excellent imitation of a British Home Stores lighting department. In addition to the sitting rooms with their collectables there is a plain front bar and a back room with pine benches for those less in need of visual stimulation. Outside there are a couple of tables right by the back door of the pub, and several more on the far side of the car park, with fairy lights for summer evenings and (were it not for the trees!) a fine view across the water to Port Penrhyn. Just round the corner is Bangor's beautifully restored Victorian pier, stretching halfway across the Menai Strait to Anglesey and now with kiosks, restaurants, amusements and a wonderful view. The views are excellent, too, from the road which runs south of the pier to Upper Bangor and the Menai Bridge.

BARMOUTH
Tal-y-Don

Tel: (0341) 280508
St Anne's Square, High Street
(A496)

✖ lunchtime and evening

🍴

◎

⛏

◁ Burtonwood Bitter

Opinions differ on Barmouth, a bustling seaside resort which is too commercialised for some but which certainly offers all the usual seaside attractions: a big sandy beach; a promenade which is part funfair, with donkey rides and fairground, and part formal gardens; and a harbour which is alive with yachts and fishing boats. The town centre, all cafes, craft centres and novelty shops, is less attractive. Those seeking to escape can do so easily, however, up the mountainside past Dinas Oleu, the National Trust's first purchase, to Diffwys and the other peaks of the southern Rhinogs, or to the Mawddach estuary, with its marvellous scenery and half-mile pedestrian bridge alongside the Cambrian Coast railway. Before they escape, though, they should try the Tal-y-Don, a solid three-storey Victorian hotel right in the middle of town. The heart of the place is the half-timbered brassy bar with its big front windows and cosmopolitan feel. There is also a more sedate lounge at the back, together with a really big garden, much of it shielded from the weather by perspex roofs and all of it, as with the rest of the pub, available for diners: food plays an important role here.

BEAUMARIS
George &
Dragon

Tel: (0248) 810491
Church Street

✖ lunchtime

◁ Robinson Best Bitter, Old Tom
(winter)

The George and Dragon is tucked away up a side street, not far from the Olde Bull's Head (see next entry), which is perhaps better known but which the "George" claims to predate. The sign over the door emphasises the claim: "This house is one of the oldest inns in Wales, and scheduled as one of the ancient buildings of Anglesey". The date in question is 1410, and the back wall of the pub is said to be part of the town's original wall. A further story has it that records exist of a court martial of Cromwell's troops found drunk on the premises. The pub boasts a collection of 460 bank notes from all over the world, and those with decent eyesight can also read a small-print account of the Battle of Trafalgar on the front page of The Times dated 7th November 1805. There is a heavily timbered ceiling in the main bar, which also serves a separate room where a large recess apparently contained one of the original fireplaces. Apart from a supporting timber beam, nothing else remains of the fireplace, and winter warmth is now assured by gas fired central heating and by the small cask of Robinson's Old Tom draught barley wine which appears on the bar late in Autumn. Apart from Old Tom and Best Bitter the "natural" beer includes bottle-conditioned Worthington White Shield.

Olde Bull's Head

Tel : (0248) 810329
Castle Street

✗ lunchtime and evening

▰

🍺 **Draught Bass**

Beaumaris, the prettiest of Anglesey's towns, is full of interesting old buildings, not least the exquisite moated castle. Not all of them, however, have the added attraction of serving Draught Bass, a long-term resident in the hotel. The Bull's Head is a Grade II listed building dating from 1472, though it was rebuilt in 1617 and was Cromwell's headquarters when his men besieged – but fortunately failed to damage – the nearby castle in 1645. The sense of history is everywhere: the courtyard at the rear is approached through the original stagecoach entrance, with the largest single-hinged door in Britain, while the oak-beamed bar with its large brick fireplace contains a fascinating collection of weapons, armour, china and brassware. There is a seventeenth-century water clock, and you can even sit in a high-backed chair which was formerly the ducking stool for the town's criminal fraternity. Locals and visitors alike come to sample the Bass, especially during regatta fortnight, though much of the conversation in the bar then is nautical in flavour and un-intelligible to the uninitiated. There is a wide range of food available, from snacks in the bar to full scale à la carte meals in the restaurant (open for lunches and evening meals every day); local sea food and game are available in season. The bedrooms have been refurbished in recent years and now offer extremely comfortable accommodation; residents are in illustrious company, both Charles Dickens and Dr Johnson having stayed in this, the town's original posting house.

BEDDGELERT
Prince Llewelyn
Hotel

Tel: (076 686) 242
Smith Street (A498)

✘ lunchtime and evening

🕭

◎

⋈

🍺 **Robinson Best Mild, Best Bitter**

One of three Robinson's pubs in the little mountain village of Beddgelert (the others, both worth a try, are the Tanronen just across the river bridge and the Saracen's Head along the street); such a near-monopoly so far from the brewery must be unique. The Prince Llewelyn is a venerable stone-built hotel, its severe appearance tempered by a portrait of the Welsh prince himself and by greenery climbing the walls in front, right by the old and narrow bridge over the sparkling waters of the Afon Colwyn. The home-cooked food and modern accommodation are exactly what is needed by the walkers who tend to be thick on the ground around here – many of them fresh from an assault on Snowdon, which rises to the north-east of the village. Beddgelert translates as "Gelert's grave"; according to legend the Gelert in question was a wolfhound mistakenly killed by Prince Llewelyn after it had saved his baby son from a wolf. A pleasant, compact stone and slate village, Beddgelert is also the site of the second oldest monastery in Wales, though virtually nothing of this remains above ground. Outstanding scenery lies to the south, through the Pass of Aberglaslyn, and to the north-east, over the Nantgwynant Pass to Llynnau Mwmbyr (for the best view of the Snowdon group) and Capel Curig.

BENLLECH BAY
Glanrafon Hotel

Tel : (0248) 852687
On the A5025

✗ lunchtime and evening

🍴

◎

ⱨ

🍺 **Lees Bitter**

The Glanrafon is centrally situated in this popular Anglesey resort, a few minutes from the fine sandy beach and even closer to the shops. There is a comfortable lounge, a good sized bar and games room, and a separate children's room. The regular clientele is an interesting mix of locals, hotel residents and visitors, and in the bar the atmosphere is more that of a local pub than a residential hotel. The beer is from John Willie Lees, a family brewery from north Manchester,

and it is worth noting that the handpumped bitter is some 15 to 20 pence cheaper here than pretty well anywhere else on the Island. Also available in bottle is naturally conditioned Worthington White Shield together with two of Lees' specials – the powerful Moonraker strong ale, and Vintage Harvest Ale, which you must ask for. This is produced each year from the new season's harvest of barley and hops, and is exceptionally strong (and also expensive, though at an original gravity of 1124 degrees you may well consider it worth the price). The well-equipped bedrooms are bright and airy, and most have magnificent sea views; the hotel makes an ideal base for a holiday. A varied programme of entertainment goes on throughout the summer months.

BETHESDA
Douglas Arms

Tel: (0248) 600219
High Street (A5)

▨

◎

ﾒ

⊕ Marston Mercian Mild, Burton Best Bitter, Pedigree; M & B Brew XI

For once the overworked epithet "unique" is fully deserved – indeed "bizarre" might be just as appropriate to describe this basic, slightly scruffy but lovable free house which has been run by the Davies family with determined eccentricity for over 50 years now. Conspicuously sited on the Betws-y-Coed to Bangor road, and a popular haunt of climbers fresh from the crags, the hotel has green-painted doors, hydrangeas and geraniums in a narrow front border, and a large entrance hall with ancient chests on either side. There are three rooms, one dominated by a full-sized snooker table which (I kid you not) has an extra ball – purple – scoring eight points. In addition there's a plain back room, with spartan decoration, and a slightly more comfortable front lounge. The central bar servery boasts a cash register which still operates with real money – pounds, shillings and pence, the currency with which the locals pay for their beer. The gardens, backing onto the Afon Ogwen, are superb, all the more so since they are unexpected in the workaday environment of Bethesda, an uncompromising slaters' village born out of the success of the Penrhyn quarries whose waste heaps dominate the landscape up-valley. Purists will love the Douglas Arms, a relic of times past which adds colour to the generally drab pub scene hereabouts; but don't take anyone weaned on plush theme pubs!

Glanrafon Hotel:
A pint of Lees
from Jim

BETWS-Y-COED
Pont-y-Pair
Hotel

Tel: (06902) 407
On the A5

✗ lunchtime and evening

🍴

◎

ᴍ

🍺 Whitbread Trophy, Castle
    Eden Ale

Stone-built and solid as the local granite, the Pont-y-Pair is an exemplary small hotel astride the main tourist route through Snowdonia. A meeting place for locals as well as visitors, the hotel offers quizzes and live music amongst the attractions in the large wrap-round lounge bar. There is also a welcome for families, and for diners either in the bar itself or in the hotel's grill room, which has a large variety of tempting dishes available. The beer is only Whitbread, however – at least for the moment. Betws, a favourite spot for walkers and canoeists, is set in delightful wooded countryside near the con-fluence of the Conwy, Llugwy and Lledr; many attractive walks can be enjoyed in the sur-rounding Gwydyr Forest. The village, hardly more than a scattered hamlet in 1801, developed rapidly after the Beaver Bridge was built across the Conwy just above the village; in 1808 the Irish Mail was diverted from the North Wales coast route to the faster route through Snow-donia. By 1884 there were six inns, including the Swan, later renamed the Pont-y-Pair simply because of its location opposite the five-arched late medieval bridge of that name. The bridge (its name translates, very aptly, as "Bridge of the Cauldron") spans the Llugwy as it foams down rocky waterslides; occasionally salmon can be seen leaping upstream in the evenings.

BODEDERN
Crown Hotel

Tel: (0407) 740734
Church Street (B5109, one mile from the A5025)

✗ lunchtime and evening

🍴

◎

ᴍ

🍺 Burtonwood Bitter

The Crown is a fine example of a small village pub with a few letting bedrooms, and has long been a favourite haunt of visitors to Anglesey whether on business or on holiday. It's about a mile off the A5025, which serves as Anglesey's northern ring road, and since it is also close to the A5, which crosses the island, it makes an excellent touring base. Activities available locally include skin diving and lake and river fishing, and there is a thousand acres of rough shooting on the doorstep. The wood beamed lounge has a stone-built fireplace and there is a pleasant bar/games room, together with a separate children's room. The accommodation is simply but comfortably furnished and very competitively priced, and a wide range of equally good value bar food is on offer. The Crown also has regular live entertainment, especially on Thursday nights. It is a notable community pub, too, and has always been high up on the list of fundraisers for a variety of deserving causes. The favourite charity used to be Guide Dogs for the Blind, but now it's Muscular Dystrophy; the Crown was recently judged top collector in Wales.

CAERNARFON
Black Boy

Tel: (0286) 3604
27 Northgate Street

✗ lunchtime and evening

☗

⌘

🍺 **Draught Bass**

A big sign covers the upper part of one wall of the Black Boy, advertising this "free, fully licensed commercial and family hotel" to tourists walking around Caernarfon's magnificent town walls, which are only yards away at the bottom of the ancient, narrow Northgate Street. The inn was built in the early sixteenth century, and underwent a thorough restoration in the 1950s though this left undisturbed the consciously "old world" atmosphere of the place, which is now nurtured carefully: even the restaurant has an inglenook fireplace. The taproom is large, with a partly quarry-tiled floor, old-fashioned bench style seating around the walls, a beamed ceiling (the beams black, the rest of it red!) and stone walls. Hatch service supplies drinkers in the area beyond the darts board. The lounge is smaller and undoubtedly the centre of attraction; by no means plush, it is nevertheless full of character, with an old stone fireplace, antique clock and many other artefacts. The bar counter itself, in dark wood but with the optics glittering brightly behind, is just right too; the few bar stools are usually claimed early on. Well provided with little corners for private conversations, the lounge is very heavily used by locals as well as summer visitors. The beer range is disappointing – in the old days Border beers were available here too – but the atmosphere is terrific.

Palace Vaults

Tel: (0286) 2093
Castle Ditch

✗ lunchtime and evening

⊕ **Marston Burton Best Bitter, Pedigree, Owd Rodger** (winter)

Very easy to find – simply aim for the spectacular castle: the Palace Vaults lies immediately opposite! – this is justifiably one of the most popular pubs in Caernarfon. The setting is remarkable, with one of the greatest medieval castles in Europe across Castle Ditch, the quay and waterfront around the corner, and, behind, the maze of narrow streets within Caernarfon's impressive town walls. The Palace has undergone quite a transformation, too, from a rather seedy but lively and likeable basic locals' bar in the 1970s to the comfortable pub with a much more cosmopolitan appeal which greets drinkers nowadays. It is, in fact, an excellent example of how to spruce up a pub without destroying its character or appeal. Essentially the pub now consists of one very large wrap-around lounge bar, but it is cleverly divided into distinct sections. At one end, the walls are lined with bookshelves, and the emphasis is on quiet enjoyment of the Marston's ales; then there is the main section where the serious drinking is done in a convivial, slightly noisy and somewhat smokey atmosphere; further round, up a few steps, is another area for the more sedate, with long leather settees, low tables, and subdued prints on the walls; and finally, beyond a fireplace whose mantleshelf carries an ancient clock, a games area with darts board caters for those of more sporting bent. The whole pub works outstandingly well; still a little boisterous at times, perhaps, but catering properly (as every good pub should) for a very wide mix of customers.

CEMAES BAY
Stag

Tel : (0407) 710281
High Street (A5025)

✘ lunchtime and evenings

🕮

☺

🍺 **Burtonwood Bitter**

Cemaes Bay is a picturesque fishing village situated on the northern tip of Anglesey, and so the Stag claims with some justification to be the most northerly pub in Wales. A white-painted building at one end of the High Street, it is only a minute or so from the beach and the bay, with its delightfully rugged scenery. All through the summer the Stag is virtually lost behind a profusion of hanging baskets and flower tubs; but in front of the pub there is a small area with tables and chairs which is ideal for enjoying a pint of Burtonwood bitter and watching the world go by. The pub is far larger than it looks from the outside – there is a long narrow lounge, a separate middle bar with a darts board, and then, up a few steps, a top bar with pool table, where families are welcome. There are old photographs of the village as it was, with the local lifeboat and ships in the harbour, contrasting with present-day colour photographs, including the air-sea rescue helicopter on exercise with the Holyhead lifeboat. The bar food available includes vegetarian dishes, while locally-caught lobster and other seafood delicacies are on the menu in season. The pub is used by locals and tourists alike, the latter including "yachties" who are prone to moor in the bay on their progress around the island – if you fancy a sail or a fishing trip yourself, just ask at the bar!

CHWILOG
Madryn Arms

Tel : (076 668) 250
High Street (A4354)

✘ lunchtime and evening

🕮

☺

🍺 **Burtonwood Dark Mild, Bitter**

Unpretentious, plain and certainly not yet spoiled by over-enthusiastic renovation, the Madryn Arms is a very good village pub catering for residents of this quite large village, tourists in general, and escapees from the huge holiday camp near Pwllheli in particular. The signing on the building is in the brewery's old style – Forshaw's Burtonwood Ales are proudly advertised – and the building itself carries its date of construction, 1868, prominently on the gable end. Now a single room, converted from separate little bars on either side of the entrance passage, the Madryn has wooden benches and tables catering for the lively local trade, and a separate family room. A good selection of meals is provided, from standard pub fare and steaks to cod kiev and lasagne verdi, while beef in real ale also features on the menu. Children have their own menu to choose from. In the garden there are rustic benches and an excellent children's playground with big wooden play equipment. As well as Pwllheli, visitors can quickly get to Criccieth, with its sheltered harbour and beach, together with a thirteenth-century castle (sacked and burned by Owain Glyndwr in 1404) set on a rocky peninsula with marvellous views over Tremadog Bay.

CONWY
Castle Hotel

Tel: (049 263) 2324
High Street

✗ lunchtime and evening

◎

⋈

🍺 **Draught Bass**

Parts of the Castle Hotel date back to the fifteenth century, though it seems to have found its niche as a superior coaching house in the early nineteenth century; now it's a Trusthouse Forte hotel of some standing. The Castle Bar, used by locals as a convenient and comfortable meeting place, has window seats (ideal for keeping an eye on life in the town centre) with low tables, and a selection of unusual paintings. Many of these were painted by John Dawson-Watson in return for board and lodgings; the most interesting, perhaps, is the "unfinished" picture which remained in that state because the painter came into an inheritance. For those wanting more than a bar meal the Shakespeare restaurant is available, specialising in fresh fish dishes including Conwy mussels and salmon in season. Visitors needing no more than a glass of Bass are equally welcome, however. Despite the name of the hotel it is actually some distance from the spectacular castle majestically sited above the Conwy estuary; somewhat closer is the quayside, alive with small boats, usually thronged with tourists (some attracted by " Britain's smallest house") and abruptly terminated to the north by the crumbling medieval walls of this fascinating town, the best preserved and most historically worthwhile in North Wales.

Tired hiker – the Prince Llewelyn

CORRIS
Slater's Arms

Tel: (0654) 73324
Lower Corris (off the A487)

✗ lunchtime

🍺 **Banks Mild Ale, Bitter**

Outwardly just a plain pub on a street corner in Corris, the Slater's Arms is a wonderfully friendly old-fashioned two-bar pub in a former slating village right next to the southern boundary of the Snowdonia National Park. From the A487 the way lies past the Corris Institute, half-timbered and with a massive clock overhanging the road, and then past signs to the Corris railway museum. The museum, housing a collection of equipment, mementoes and pictures relating to the Corris Railway, which served the Dulas valley between Machynlleth and Aberllefenni for almost a hundred years, is a marvellous example of a small private collection made available to the public. The Slater's Arms is almost in the same category. It is exactly as a village pub should be, its bar well scrubbed and homely, with big settles and sporting photographs around a huge fireplace. The fireplace, a source of some pride, has assorted bric-a-brac on the mantleshelf and is decorated with moulded bunches of grapes. An almost separate back room houses a piano and still more photographs of local life, concentrating particularly on schoolchildren. A completely separate lounge is quieter but perhaps has less character. As for the slate workings, they are surprisingly well hidden in the upper valley, but nevertheless pretty devastating in their impact on the local landscape.

DOLGELLAU
Royal Ship

Tel: (0341) 422209
Bridge Street

✗ lunchtime and evening

🛏

🍺 **Robinson Best Bitter**

A coaching inn of relatively recent pedigree – built in 1813, though much extended and repeatedly modernised since then – the Royal Ship is a very prominent building in Dolgellau, its virginia creeper covered facade squarely in view of every driver travelling northwards through this likeable market town. Below the creeper is a very white porch and a cobbled patio with a few tables, notable for their view of the extensive, corrugated northern buttresses of Cader Idris, not the highest but perhaps the most exciting of the Welsh mountains (try the Minfordd path!) but otherwise a little too close to the insistent traffic for comfort. Quite a number of bars are available to the visitor to this welcoming, well-appointed hotel. To the right of the entrance hall is a snug little lounge bar, comfortably furnished enough but somehow appearing rather dated; to the left is a further lounge much in demand with those requiring food. Bar snacks and full meals are usually available, and indeed the accent is very much on food, though the Robinson's beer is also given due attention. Curiously, there is an entirely separate entrance, on the Bridge Street side of the hotel, to a plain public bar and yet another lounge bar, this one rather less plush than those at the front.

Stag

Tel: (0341) 422533
Bridge Street

✘ lunchtime

🏠

🍺 **Burtonwood Dark Mild, Bitter**

An archetypal town pub close to the seventeenth-century bridge which, until the by-pass was opened, shepherded northbound traffic out of the town, the Stag is very well known to regular travellers in this part of the world as the ideal spot to break a long journey. There is only a single bar, and not a particularly big one at that, but the welcome is warm and genuine and the beer seldom less than superb. Full of character and with a real community spirit, the Stag is a very popular darts pub (the Stag Ladies are the current Gwynedd super league champions and the trophy cabinet is bursting full) even though the darts board can only just be squeezed into the available space. There are only a few benches and tables – some of them tucked under the large inglenook fireplace – but the very lack of space somehow reinforces the cheerful atmosphere and timeless Welsh character of the place. The food consists of a variety of honest, good-value pub snacks. Well-hidden at the back of the pub is a patio with picnic tables, tubs of flowers and fairy lights for summer evenings. Along the lane from here is the start of a delightful stroll among the little back streets of Dolgellau, with its neat houses, old-fashioned shops and old tannery right by the bridge. Friday is the time to come, when the market is in full swing: so too, as the day wears on, is the Stag!

DOLWYDDELAN
Gwydyr

Tel: (06906) 209
On the A470

✗ lunchtime and evening

🍴

🛏

🍺 Tetley Bitter

Although the Gwydyr merits inclusion in this guide largely because of its superb location for those touring Snowdonia, this cosy little pub opposite the church in the centre of the typically North Walian village of Dolwyddelan, deep in the Lledr valley south of Betws-y-Coed, has its own intrinsic attractions. A solid two-storey inn decked out in Allied Breweries' livery and with well-tended flower borders adding to its visual appeal, it is surprisingly accessible by public transport, with the scenic Llandudno Junction to Blaenau Ffestiniog railway running close by. The bars are welcoming and brassy, and there is plenty of room to sit and drink outside, with shaded picnic tables to one side and a slightly unkempt garden to the rear. The Banks's beer has gone, however, and the Tetley's hasn't quite the same *cachet*. Welsh is spoken in the bars as a matter of course, but visitors are soon made to feel at home too. Higher up the valley is the impressive Dolwyddelan Castle, the thirteenth-century stronghold of the Welsh princes. Reputedly the birthplace of Llywelyn the Great, it is now reduced to a 40-foot tower rising bleakly against bare hillslopes. Further south are the slate mines of Blaenau Ffestiniog, now somewhat prettified for visitors but still an awesome sight.

DULAS
Pilot Boat

Tel : (024 888) 205
On the A5025

✗ lunchtime and evening

🍴

©

🍺 **Robinson Best Mild, Best Bitter**

The Pilot Boat is a friendly, welcoming white-painted Robinson's house nestling in a hollow below but just visible from the A5025 about halfway between Benllech and Amlwch, at what is still called City Dulas on some maps. Like many Anglesey pubs it finds its regular local clientele much boosted by visitors on any fine weekend, particularly during the summer months. The main entrance to the pub leads straight into the bar; there is a small lounge leading off it, and a separate games/pool room. Both lounge and pool room double as family rooms. There is also a small but pleasant garden area, boasting some particularly fine views. The main bar has a flagged floor and wood-beamed ceiling, a stone fireplace and a collection of banknotes from around the world; the main theme, however, is unashamedly nautical, with pictures of ships, navigation lights and – somewhat more unusually – the bar itself fashioned from part of a small clinker-built boat. The Pilot Boat offers an excellent range of good-value food, including some children's specialities. Only two miles to the east is a fascinating area, well worth strolling around to work up a thirst, with the remains of the walled Iron Age village of Din Llugwy, the roofless medieval chapel of Capel Llugwy and a burial chamber dating from around 3000 BC. An alternative destination is Ynys Dulas, the haunt of grey seals.

DWYGYFYLCHI
Fairy Glen

Tel: (0492) 3316
At the bottom of the Sychnant Pass

✕ lunchtime

🍴

🍺 Marston Mercian Mild, Pedigree

The *cognoscenti* already go this way to avoid the traffic problems on the A55 while the Conwy tunnel is under construction. Those in search of a decent pint in pleasant surroundings should do the same, for this is an excellent wayside pub in a rather sprawling village at the beginning (or preferably the end!) of the narrow, winding road leading over the Sychnant Pass, and rising above a steep-sided heather-clad gorge of breathtaking beauty. A strikingly white pub, with details picked out in a rather severe green and rocky hillslopes rising immediately behind, the Fairy Glen (the name refers to the well-wooded rocky ravine) has a few benches and tables in front, together with hanging baskets and flower tubs. The lounge bar has window seats, nooks and crannies, tables in an old inglenook and plenty of greenery including a profusion of plants on an old sideboard. The walls are enlivened with a collection of plates and sundry advertisements for Nixey's Black Lead and Borax amongst others, though the sepia-toned photographs above the bar – including one of a horse and cart descending Sychnant Pass – are of greater intrinsic interest. A side room has more tables but seems to be provided largely for the benefit of the darts fraternity.

FAIRBOURNE
Fairbourne Hotel

Tel: (0341) 250203
Off the A493

✕ lunchtime and evening

🍴

◎

🛏

🍺 McEwan 70/-, Younger IPA

Fairbourne is possibly one of those places which is at its best when viewed from afar, in this case from the hills to the south, with the long sandy beach in front of the colourwashed houses of the village, the railway viaduct over the picturesque Mawddach estuary, and the southern bastions of the Rhinogs, one of the least well-known mountain ranges in Snowdonia. The village itself is unspectacular, but the Fairbourne Hotel, 300 years old and standing in its own grounds at the entrance to Fairbourne and close to the railway station, must be exempted from any general criticism. It is a large, well-appointed and comfortable hotel, well placed for exploring the coast and the mountains, with excellent food in generous proportions, well-kept beer and pleasant surroundings to drink it in. The lounge bar is attractive, long and narrow, with subdued lighting and plenty of quiet corners; outside the terrace, with white tables and chairs in front of trim lawns and shrubs, has breath-taking views over the estuary. The narrow gauge railway, a former tramway running from the village to Penrhyn Point, right at the end of a sandspit in the Mawddach estuary and with ferry services to Barmouth, is the smallest of the Great Little Trains of Wales and offers an outstanding way to spend the afternoon.

Fairy Glen at Dwygyfylchi

GLYNGARTH
Gazelle

Tel: (0248) 713364
On the A545

✗ lunchtime and evening

🍴 Robinson Best Bitter, Old Tom (winter)

The Gazelle is a residential inn beautifully situated below terraced gardens, right on the shores of the Menai Strait. From here there is a panoramic view sweeping round from Great Orme's Head along the Strait, with the mountains of Snowdonia as a backdrop, to Telford's suspension bridge at Menai Bridge. It is an ideal spot to watch the Straits Regatta which takes place during the first two weeks in August – and if, at a slightly less exalted level, you want to have a go yourself, sailing fishing and watersports can be arranged. The Gazelle has a sizeable and attractive main bar and a number of other rooms ideal for a quiet drink or for accommodating children. All these rooms and alcoves are comfortably furnished and there is the inevitable profusion of maritime prints and photographs. The food is good and the menu wide-ranging (children are not forgotten), both in the bar and in the separate restaurant. An especially delightful feature is that all the public rooms have views across the Menai Strait to Bangor Pier, recently refurbished and a growing tourist attraction in its own right. The bedrooms are comfortable, but the real attraction is the prospect of waking up to the mouth-watering prospect of the Welsh mountains seemingly within touching distance across the water – provided, of course, that the rain holds off!

LLANBEDR
Victoria

Tel: (034 123) 213
On the A496

✗ lunchtime and evening

🍴 Robinson Best Mild, Best Bitter

Tucked away on the coast road south of Harlech, Llanbedr is a fine base for exploring the area: the seashore (including Mochras or Shell Island, with 200 different varieties of shells); the countryside, with a nature trail in Cwm Nantcol and a farm trail at Cefn Isaf; and the Rhinogs, with the so-called "Roman Steps" above Cwm Bychan a much-used way to the main ridge. The Victoria, stone-built but its lines softened by rambling roses, sits right in the centre of Llanbedr on the banks of the Artro, and is an excellent hostelry, both for those staying in the area and those in need of a meal or drink. The bars are really delightful, with the Settle Bar especially full of character. This has beamed ceilings, an inglenook with an original kitchen range, its main beam adorned with horse brasses, a strange circular wooden settle, a grandfather clock and many other artefacts. The lounge bar, light and spacious, also has beams and brasses and an attractive fireplace. A special feature is the sheltered garden, with plenty of tables on a manicured lawn, and a children's play area including swings, slides and a wendy house. The bedrooms (all en-suite) are pleasantly furnished: the Victoria may no longer be a coaching inn but it remains dedicated to providing every comfort for travellers.

Detail of the Gazelle,

LLANBEDROG
Glyn-y-Weddw
Arms

Tel: (0758) 740212
Lower Village

✗ lunchtime and evening

𐄂

◎

🍺 Robinson Best Mild, Best
Bitter, Old Tom (winter)

This well-kept seaside village local is deservedly one of the most praised pubs in one of the nicest parts of the Lleyn peninsula, with excellent food, a popular family room and an attractive and fairly spacious outside seating area which understandably has a well-populated if somewhat frenetic feel to it on sunny summer days. The Robinson's beer, a long way from home here (and, rather surprisingly, not to everyone's taste in deepest Gwynedd) is seldom less than extremely quaffable, and the food on offer is very varied and much appreciated by the holidaymakers. The bars are comfortable and welcoming and the whole atmosphere of the pub is very well-managed. Highly accessible from the sheltered, sandy and very pretty tree-fringed beach, which is perfect for families with its safe bathing, the Glyn-y-Weddw is also close to the restored village church in its sylvan setting. The church is approached through a tiny lych-gate; note also the carved screen and unusual minstrel's gallery. The whole village lies below a sheer and very well-wooded cliff and is thus very well shielded from the prevailing south-westerly winds. Further south, beyond Plas Glyn-y-Weddw, is the little cone-shaped hill of Mynydd Tirycwmwd, thrusting out into Cardigan Bay and with outstanding views across the waters into the distant heart of Snowdonia.

Ship

Tel: (0758) 740270
Bryn-y-Gro (B4413)

✗ lunchtime and evening

𐄂

🍺 Burtonwood Dark Mild, Bitter

Slightly removed from the seashore in this crowded honeypot of a village – and none the worse for that – the Ship is an old, cosy and friendly pub popular with both locals and visitors. It draws customers from the whole of Lleyn with its well-kept Burtonwood beer and ambitious food. An extensive selection of bar food is available, with over thirty salads and hot meals. There are two bars, with their own individual characteristics but sharing a delightfully informal atmosphere. The public bar is particularly notable, both for the pub games played with such obvious enthusiasm by the locals, and for the resoundingly friendly spirit which pervades the place. There is also an excellent suntrap garden just right for a summer drink. The Ship is not just a watering hole for those visiting Llanbedrog but also a marvellous centre for the western (and most unspoilt) part of Lleyn. Bardsey Island, with the remains of Wales's oldest monastery; the rugged Irish sea coastline; and the bleak unspoilt Porth Neigwl (Hell's Mouth) are all within easy reach. Even closer is the old mill on Foel Fawr, now in the care of the National Trust, which gives a magnificent view over four counties and – on a clear day – the Wicklow Mountains in Ireland.

LLANBEDR Y CENNIN
Olde Bull Inn

Tel: (049 269) 508
Half a mile from the B5106

✗ lunchtime and evening

🍴

◎

⊨

🍺 Lees GB Mild, Bitter

St Peter's village of the leeks (in rather rough-and-ready translation), Llanbedr is beautifully situated below the northern outposts of the Carneddau. Packhorse trails head westward for Tal-y-bont and Bangor, while the main Conwy valley roads are a little distance away to the east, giving the old village a very tranquil air. The Bull Inn sits well with this apparent peacefulness, though this was not always the case, for the old inn was the focal point of Llanbedr Fair (Ffair Lambed) every October. Colourful and rumbustious, the fair marked the beginning of winter; the end of Ffair Lambed was the signal for the putting in of the cows throughout the valley. Not so any more, though the Bull remains, a whitewashed stone sixteenth-century building with a giant pictorial inn sign on one wall and with a lovely position above the Conwy valley. It's a splendid local with an unspoilt interior including a dining room notable for its exposed timbers rescued from an Armada wreck. The menu is extensive and features home cooking seven days a week, and do-it-yourself barbecues are also available for parties (phone for details). Well-behaved children are welcome too, and the accommodation is popular, not least with those intent on conquering some of the Snowdonian peaks; the path to Foel Grach and Carnedd Llewelyn starts close to the Bull.

LLANDUDNO
Cottage Loaf

Tel: (0492) 70762
Market Street

✗ lunchtime

◎ until 8 pm

◫ **Ruddles Best Bitter, County: Webster Yorkshire Bitter, Choice**

Aptly known as the "village pub in the heart of town", the Cottage Loaf is a welcome resting place for locals and visitors alike in this bustling seaside resort, now an important shopping centre as well as an elegant holiday base with pier, promenade, beaches and plenty of entertainments. Surprisingly the pub was extensively rebuilt only eight years ago, having previously served as an old bakery (hence the pub's name); only the old cellars survive, though the old ships' masts which support the roof are also remnants of the bakery. The flagstone floors are another nice touch in such a recent arrival on the scene. All the real ales are from subsidiaries of Grand Metropolitan, which is a pity despite the presence of Ruddles County, one of the better known real ales. The lunchtime food is, however, excellent, with a menu which varies from day to day but has an emphasis on freshly-made wholesome food and a welcome absence of chips. As an added bonus pizzas with fresh toppings are served from noon throughout the day (the pub takes full advantage of the new licensing laws). The "Loaf" has live music twice a week, on Tuesdays and Sundays, and on Wednesdays there is a quiz night with the distinctly useful first prize of 22 pints of the winner's choice.

London Hotel

Tel: (0492) 76740
131 Mostyn Street

✗ lunchtime and evening

☺

⋈

⊲ **Burtonwood Dark Mild, Bitter**

One block away from the sea, Mostyn Street is the main shopping thoroughfare of Llandudno, with iron-and-glass arcades providing a fittingly Victorian stylish touch. In the middle of one such arcade towards the top of the street is the London Hotel, attractively green-painted and sporting a Dick Whittington inn sign. The overall design of the pub is unusual, and there are oddities inside too, with an old red telephone box emphasising the metropolitan theme of the place. Usually busy, especially for its lunchtime meals, the London has a big central bar serving a number of different lounge areas, including a particularly cosy corner to the left of the main passageway. At the back of the pub is a really excellent family room which is transformed into a piano bar in the evenings. The London hosts a folk club every Saturday night, and a very contented crowd of drinkers on most other nights of the week. Lunchtime drinkers can spill out later to do their shopping on Mostyn Street, named after Lord Mostyn, who laid out the town in 1849 behind the curving beach linking the Great and Little Ormes, two limestone headlands. Just around the corner is the quintessentially Victorian pier and promenade, while beyond the pier is the Happy Valley, carefully landscaped and offering views along the promenade to the Little Orme.

Olde Victoria

Tel: (0492) 860949
Church Walks

✗ lunchtime and evening

⊕

⊲ **Theakston Best Bitter, Old Peculier; Younger IPA, No. 3**

A very comfortable pub in a street of big terraced houses just off the town centre, with a reputation for good food and a wide range of real ales (admittedly all from various bits of Scottish & Newcastle). Essentially there is one big room, though it's well divided and indeed Albert's Pantry, with its red check tablecloths, is virtually separate. The central bar is attractively constructed of dark wood, with plenty of bar stools for the more extrovert, while for less gregarious souls there are seats in a variety of styles, including soft settees, in the windows and around the walls of the lounge. The walls are decorated with a large and impressive collection of Victorian photographs of Llandudno – perhaps in its heyday then – although the old queen herself looks down, disapprovingly of course, on the goings-on of the present day. There are plenty of potted plants around the place, even in the well-appointed loos. In front of the pub is a patio for warmer days in summer. At one end of the street lies the promenade, at the other lies the top of the shopping centre, but in Church Walks itself a calmer atmosphere prevails; it, and the Olde Victoria, are well worth seeking out.

LLANGEFNI
Railway Inn

Tel : (0248) 722166
High Street

✘ lunchtime

🏠

☺

🍺 Lees GB Mild, Bitter

The Railway stands at the top of the High Street in Llangefni, and is a good example of the "many different rooms" genre. There is a passageway leading directly from the entrance door to the end of the bar, with a small cosy lounge to one side. The rest of the pub consists of a number of different drinking areas, some simply alcoves, with a separate games room and, behind the bar, yet another room which is partly built into the rising ground on which the pub stands. The builders moved in during 1989 and sparked fears that major alterations might be in hand. "It's not going to change much" said the landlord, gazing at a scene of total devastation; remarkably, it seems that he was right, and to Lees' credit the separate rooms have largely been retained. The rising ground has now been turned into a feature of the pub, with natural rock picked out by spotlight. Handpumped Lees' beers are available together with a good selection of fairly uncomplicated bar food. The Railway is very much a locals' pub, which tends sometimes to be overlooked by visitors because of its situation well away from the main shopping area and the large car park (itself covered by stalls on market days). The Thursday market is particularly popular, and well worth attending – but for a quiet pint away from the bargain-hunters the Railway is the place.

NEVER ON A SUNDAY

Sign in the Prince Llewellyn

LLWYNGWRIL
Garthangarad

Tel: (0341) 250240
On A493

✗ lunchtime and evening

☺

Ⓗ

🍺 **Banks Mild Ale, Bitter**

The Garthangarad, a real haven at the top of the older part of Llwyngwril, with its low stone houses and little lanes, is a little whitewashed pub close to the footpath leading to an uncrowded and scenic beach, with its panorama of Cardigan Bay. Further north, as the village sprawls out, there are outstanding views across the Mawddach estuary to Barmouth and the Rhinogs, though to the south the prospect is compromised somewhat by the huge and conspicuous Gwril caravan park. Above the door of the Garthangarad is a brass plate indicating that the pub was once tied to the City Brewery Company of Lichfield, which clearly built up a far-flung tied estate before becoming part of Banks's empire. From the entrance hall a sliding door to the right gives access to a tiny and very cosy lounge, while on the left is a plain but much-valued family room with a few tables and some fruit machines. At the back of the pub, down some steps, is an equally plain, functional public bar. Well-kept and with quite some character, the Garthangarad is a nice place to call in for good beer and appetising food in a friendly atmosphere. The village, though, is a winner of best-kept village awards and perhaps as a consequence of this appears self-consciously pretty in places.

MAENTWROG
Grapes

Tel: (076 685) 208
On the A496

✗ lunchtime and evening

☺

Ⓗ

🍺 **Stones Best Bitter, Draught Bass**

Delightfully situated just off the fast A470 on the road to Harlech, the Grapes is a splendid old inn, acquiring its role as a posting house only in the nineteenth century but with much older parts including a thirteenth-century cellar. Celebrities to have darkened the doors include personalities as diverse as Lloyd George and Lily Langtry. Now tourists and businessmen finding themselves in the outstandingly picturesque Vale of Ffestiniog can find a modernised but characterful base here. The big old-fashioned public bar – perhaps the "magnificent parlour" where George Borrow took brandy and water on his tour of *Wild Wales* – has big old wooden gables with bench seating. Guns adorn the copper-topped bar, while there is a collection of old beer bottles on high shelving and advertisements for Sunlight Soap and the like on the walls. Darts seems to be played mostly by those who favour seven feet nine and a quarter inches as their throwing distance. The lounge bar with its notable open fire is warmly attractive, while children are welcome in a third comfortable room. The downstairs restaurant is in the oldest part of the building, with a massive slate beam over the fireplace (where the chef spit-roasts or barbecues to order!). An old range and smoker is still in place. Both here and in the bar there is a wide choice of food. And on the verandah, with a spectacular view over walled gardens to the Vale of Ffestiniog, is a shellfish and salad servery in season.

MARIANGLAS
Parciau Arms

Tel: (0248) 853766
On B5110

✗ lunchtime and evening

🍴

🍺 Banks Bitter; Ind Coope Burton Ale; occasional guest beers

The Parciau is about a mile from the main A5025 road, not far from the holiday village of Benllech; watch out for the sign on the right when approaching from this direction, since the pub is well hidden by trees. Originally the clubhouse for a caravan park, the Parciau Arms has been a fully-fledged pub for several years now, run first by father and now by son. The comfortable lounge bar, full of gleaming brass and copperware, has a small dining room leading off, while there is a separate bar and games room. The large garden area comes complete with children's play equipment, and for rainy days there is a Kids Kabin, with tables, chairs and a couple of machines. Families are made very welcome indeed; the Parciau has taken full advantage of the new all-day licensing laws, and serves morning coffees and afternoon teas as well. There is an exceptionally wide range of pub food, but it can get very busy in season – so much so that notices are posted warning of unavoidable delays at peak periods. The beers, which are quite expensive, change from time to time, though Banks's bitter and Burton Ale are the two regulars; guest beers include Draught Bass.

Copper, in the Parciau Marianglas

MENAI BRIDGE
Liverpool Arms

Tel : (0248) 712453
St Georges Pier (off the A545)

✗ lunchtime and evening

🍴

ⓐ

🍺 **Greenall's Bitter, Thomas Greenall's Original**

The Liverpool Arms is tucked away just off the main road through Menai Bridge, close to the old ferry crossing over the Menai Strait. It's an old building, full of character, and has miraculously escaped most of the periodic refurbishments which are inflicted on the majority of pubs from time to time. The main bar is relatively small and very cosy, with room for only a few tables and whose walls are covered by a vast collection of old – mainly nautical – photographs, prints, maps and charts, including one of the notorious "Swellies" in the Strait. There is a small back room, known as the Cabin, served from the same bar, and this contains a huge collection of naval artefacts including barometers and telescopes, together with more miscellaneous old items such as a copper foot-warmer. The comfortably furnished lounge has pictures of yachts and sailing ships, and there are sporting prints in the hall. A recent addition is a sun-trap of a conservatory with a wonderful display of fuschias, and there is also a small enclosed outside drinking area, as well as tables and chairs outside the pub. An excellent selection of food is served – even the ploughman's has five assorted cheeses! – and you can eat in the bar or in any of the other rooms (where, there being no bar, families can be accommodated). There is a separate dining room too. The latest real ale to appear is Thomas Greenall's Original (replacing the now defunct "original" Original), well-kept here and a worthy adjunct to the food.

MOELFRE
Kinmel Arms

Tel: (024 888 231)
On the A5108

✘ lunchtime and evening

🍴

🍺 **Robinson Best Mild, Best Bitter**

The Kinmel Arms is well placed in this small coastal village, not far from a small pebble beach, with fine sea views (sometimes with porpoises in the foreground) across to Llandudno and the Great Orme. The beers, perhaps a little over-chilled at times, are Robinson's – the mild an increasing rarity for Anglesey. The pub was once multi-roomed, with a delightful variety of little nooks and crannies, but was opened out during Robinson's "airport lounge" period of modernisation, so much so that it even has a snack bar.

Nevertheless the Kinmel Arms remains well worth visiting because of the remarkable collection of maps, photographs, charts and other information on all things maritime. It was at Moelfre that the "Royal Charter" foundered with the loss of 425 lives in 1859 while on passage from Australia to Liverpool. Often known as the "golden wreck", she was reputedly carrying bullion from the Australian goldfields. A hundred years later – to the day – the "Hindlea" was wrecked, and the crew were rescued by the Moelfre lifeboat, earning coxswain Richard Evans his second gold medal from the Royal National Lifeboat Institution for his gallantry. In 1939 the submarine "Thetis" sank in Liverpool Bay, and was later beached at nearby Traeth Bychan.

All of these happenings are documented in an impressive array of photographs, leaflets and newspaper cuttings. Other charts and diagrams cover fish, sails, knots, molluscs and crustaceans, semaphore, lifeboat stations, navigation, fishing on Anglesey, a tourist guide to Anglesey, and there are also photographs of the old village.

NANT PERIS
Vaynol Arms

Tel: (0286) 870284
On the A4086

✖ lunchtime and evening

🏠

🍺 **Robinson Best Mild, Best Bitter**

A timeless rural pub in a little hamlet up-valley from the much more tourist-hungry Llanberis, the Vaynol Arms lies below the brooding cliffs hiding the upper reaches of Snowdon, at 3560 ft the highest mountain in Wales. The situation is quite magnificent and the long low whitewashed inn fits snugly into the scene, dominating the flat meadowland but (especially when seen from across the valley) insignificant against the terrific screes and crags behind. Opposite are the equally steep lower slopes of Y Garn, with fine walking here culminating in the rocky moon-scapes around Glyder Fawr. Not surprisingly, therefore, the Vaynol's bar is very often packed with climbers and hillwalkers; both they and campers in the valley can also take advantage of the pub's sizeable camper's breakfasts, an enterprising addition to local cuisine. Later in the day there are substantial bar meals available to complement the real ale from Robinson. Lower in the valley, beyond Llyn Peris, its waters now part of the Dinorwig hydro-electric scheme, lies the village of Llanberis, with plenty for all the family to try, including two narrow-gauge railways (the Snowdon Mountain Railway, Britains only rack-and-pinion railway, offering a five-mile ride to the summit; and the Llanberis Lake Railway, on the other side of the valley), the beautifully-sited Dolbadarn Castle, the National Slate Museum, and Padarn Country Park.

NEFYN
Sportsman

Tel: (0758) 720205
Stryd Fawr (B4417)

✖ lunchtime and evening

🏠

🍺 **Tetley Bitter, Ind Coope Burton Ale**

Extremely popular with those on holiday here (and there are plenty of visitors, many of them self-catering in cottages and chalets here and in Morfa Nefyn), but also carrying on the traditions of a true Welsh local, the Sportsman is a vital component of Nefyn's High Street. This half-village, half-town with its odd, heavily restored church and more recent sprawling tourist development, has the advantages of superb, clean and sandy beaches close by. There's historical interest too, on the narrow rocky peninsula a couple of miles to the west (reached by coastal footpath across the golf course). Here is the natural harbour of Porth Dinllaen, now much in favour with yachtsmen but previously chosen – with supreme optimism – as the departure point for the Irish Mail. The remarkably straight road from Pwllheli to Nefyn was built to improve communications to this remote spot, but Porth Dinllaen was simply in the wrong place, and the scheme fell through. As a result the area retains its tranquility, not least in the Sportsman, with its very friendly reception for strangers, its cosily-furnished little lounge, and its huge wood fire, increasingly highly valued as winter draws in. There are special celebrations in the pub on saints' days too!

PENMAENMAWR
Legend

Tel: (0492) 623231
Off the A55

✗ lunchtime and evening

🍺

🍺 **Sam Powell Original; Ansells Mild, Tetley Bitter, Ind Coope Burton Ale**

Recently and very successfully refurbished, the Legend is a very good single-roomed free house in the Dwygyfylchi area of the sprawling settlement of Penmaenmawr. The A55 coast road, now much improved, is not far away, making this a very accessible local. The bar, a marvellous social centre nowadays, is interestingly decorated with a variety of mementoes and more modern artefacts, and it plays host to singalongs every Sunday and darts and pool competitions on Thursdays. Many families will be attracted by the Legend's beer garden, which comes complete with a really excellent and very popular children's play area featuring a giant dragon ride. Another attraction is the wide range of food, with bar snacks and full meals seven days a week, and a supper licence for late diners. The beer range is equally wide, with both the Sam Powell's Original and the Burton Ale (the giant Allied Breweries' only really memorable beer) both worth drinking. Oddly enough

Penmaenmawr was Gladstone's holiday haunt, but the railway and new road have between them substantially lessened the attractiveness of the seafront. More interesting (though a stiff climb) is the so-called Druid's Circle, occupied in the Bronze and Iron Ages and the site of a stone axe factory which exported its products to the whole of Britain.

Among the maps in the Liverpool Arms, Menai Bridge

PENRHYNSIDE
Cross Keys

Tel: (0492) 46415
Pendre Road

✗ lunchtime

🍴

☺

🍺 **Sam Powell's Original;
Ansells Mild, Tetley Bitter, Ind
Coope Burton Ale**

This is a really good village local: the sign of the Cross Keys shines like a beacon in this oddly suburbanised area between Llandudno and Colwyn Bay. Penrhynside itself is a tidy, well-to-do village a little removed from the main road but close to the Little Orme, the limestone headland defining the western end of Colwyn Bay. The first hostelry to be named pub of the year by the local branch of CAMRA, and deservedly so, the Cross Keys has very well-kept beer, including an excellent pint of Powell's Original (but sadly no longer any Banks's bitter!), and a good range of tasty and wholesome bar food. The rooms at the back of the pub have extensive views of the coast from the Little Orme and Penrhyn Bay eastwards, and there is also a garden and barbecue area. Children are welcome until mid-evening at the discretion of the landlord (but please confirm this first). Regular entertainment includes live music, but the real attraction of the Cross Keys is its role as the focus of community life in this old quarrying village. Of interest nearby is Penrhyn Old Hall, a Tudor manor house converted to a restaurant, while higher up the hill is Gloddaeth Hall, with another distinctive Tudor great hall.

RED WHARF BAY
Ship

Tel: (0248) 852568
One mile from the A5025

✗ lunchtime and evening

🍴

☺

🛏 (self-catering)

🍺 **Banks Bitter; Tetley Mild,
Bitter; guest beers**

Red Wharf Bay is signposted off the A5025, about a mile south of Benllech. The Ship is a long white-painted building only yards from the three-mile wide beach, with flagged floors, wood beamed ceilings, exposed stone walls and open fires. It gets extremely busy in the summer months with an influx of tourists including yachtsmen whose boats are moored in the bay. There are two main rooms, each with a bar, containing interesting naval artefacts, old china and brassware, and a little breweriana. A small children's room leads off from one bar, and a games room from the other. There is a wide range of excellent, and often adventurous, bar food on offer – Mississippi Mud Pie is one example – and much of it consists of local produce, including sea food. Indeed the Ship was highly commended after reaching the regional finals in the Guinness Pub Food awards. The restaurant upstairs is extremely popular with residents and visitors alike for a special night out. In summer visitors can sleep off the effects of too much food in the self-catering chalet accommodation. The choice of beer changes from time to time, though Tetley's mild and Banks's bitter are regulars, and there is also a dark, sweetish "house" beer called Kenneally Bitter (landlord Andrew Kenneally has been here for eighteen years) which is said to have an original gravity of 1045; further details have yet to be divulged! There is plenty of room to sit outside, and every reason to do so, with superb views across the sands to Llanddona and the open sea (cockling available to the adventurous, though the incoming tide can be dangerous).

RHOSGOCH
Rhosgoch Hotel
(The Ring)

Tel: (0407) 830720
Two miles from the B5111.
OS409892

✗ lunchtime

🛏

◎

◁ **Stones Best Bitter, Draught Bass**

The Ring has had quite a variety of owners since 1980, and the beers have varied too – first Greenalls, then Scottish & Newcastle, now Bass (the Draught Bass is very well kept, though it is a pity nothing more adventurous is available). The Ring has a small lounge/snug which also doubles (trebles?) as a dining room and family room, together with a long, narrow bar with a pool table at one end. Both rooms are warmed by roaring log fires in winter. Often quiet at lunchtime, the pub is busy at night with a mix of residents and visitors; the community singing on Fridays and Saturdays (accompanied by the organ on Saturdays) is a treat not to be missed.

There are some spectacular pictures of oil tanker fires, taken by landlord Chris Jones when he was skipper of a fire-fighting tug in the Gulf. They say that when he rings last orders on Anglesey's biggest ship's bell behind the bar, everyone in the neighbourhood knows exactly what time it is. No-one is quite sure where the alternative (and most commonly used) name of the pub originated; some say that it is derived from the cattle-ring which catered for farmers bringing their livestock to the long-defunct station nearby, whilst others have a more sinister explanation, suggesting that there used to be a cock-fighting ring here.

ROEWEN
Ty Gwyn

Tel: (0492) 650232
One mile from B5106. OS759720

✗ lunchtime

🛏

🕲

📶

🍺 Lees GB Mild, Bitter

The Ty Gwyn is a beautiful country pub only a mile from the Conwy valley road yet in a really tranquil setting. The village of Roewen, winner of the local best-kept village award and proud of it, sits neatly and tidily in its side valley, with cottages straggling up the valley into the foothills of the Carneddau. The Roman road from Canovium in the Conwy valley to Segontium (Caernarfon) passed by here, and much later, when drove roads and packhorse trails converged here, the village inn was a natural stopping point for drovers taking their cattle to market. The Ty Gwyn, a delightful white-painted cottagey building, is perfectly in keeping with the style of the village, and its inn sign, a meticulously painted reproduction of the inn, is of some merit as well. There are lots of flowers in tubs and hanging baskets around the little porch, which leads into a traditional bar, an ideal spot for an unhurried pint – except in the height of summer when it can become crowded with walkers, carborne tourists and possibly even local singers. Summer also sees barbecues in the garden, which is immediately across the road; secluded and safe behind walls and hedges, it has rustic benches and little privet hedges.

TAL-Y-CAFN
Tal-y-Cafn Hotel

Tel: (0492) 650203
Llanrwst Road (A470)

✗ lunchtime and evening

🛏

◎

⊨

🍺 **Greenall's Bitter**

A large black-and-white painted inn of no great apparent antiquity, the Tal-y-Cafn is outstandingly well placed for travellers, right on the A470 between Conwy and Llanrwst and very close to a station on British Rail's picturesque Conwy Valley line. Beyond the railway and its level crossing is the bridge over the River Conwy, here tidal and muddy. The bridge was built in 1897 as a replacement for a chain ferry – a royal ferry known in the reign of Edward I as the "passage of la Taverne". The toll house, also built in 1897, still stands, but the bridge has been toll-free since 1929, when it was jointly purchased by the former Caernarfonshire and Denbighshire county councils. The Tal-y-Cafn Hotel, splendidly welcoming and with something for everyone, has a comfortably-furnished bar with a low-beamed ceiling and an excellent beer garden, its lawns, shaded tables and a children's play area enclosed behind tall hedges. A remarkable number of guide book stickers on the well-worn entrance doors testifies to the pub's eclectic appeal. The menu is wide-ranging and represents pretty good value, and the accommodation is well worth bearing in mind for visitors to this exceptionally rewarding area.

Marina
The Liverpool Arms
Menai Bridge

TRAWSFYNNYDD
White Lion

Tel: (076 687) 277
Main Street (off the A470)

✕ lunchtime and evening

Ⓐ

⋈

🍺 Burtonwood Dark Mild, Bitter

Traditional and unspoilt, the White Lion lies right in the middle of Trawsfynydd, a big though rather ordinary village situated in a lovely mountain area but also, less congenially, very close to the ageing Trawsfynydd power station, the first inland nuclear power station in Britain. Despite its modern neighbour, the White Lion's greatest attribute is its unchanging appearance. It is a solid, basic village local with a big welcome for travellers. The clientele includes pony trekkers, walkers from the Rhinogs or from the nature trail laid out around the shores of Llyn Trawsfynydd, and fishermen – no doubt attracted by the fact that the lake temperature is slightly increased by its use in cooling the power station, so that the fish are plentiful and bigger. The centre of operations is the public bar on the right of the entrance passageway; homely, practical and quite spartan, it is a hive of activity, with pub games and plenty of conversation (much of it in Welsh). An old-fashioned lounge provides facilities for families with children. On the far side of the A470 is Tomen y Mur, a medieval castle mound on the site of a Roman camp: the route of Sarn Helen, the Roman road which ran down the western side of Wales, passes close by here.

TREFRIW
Olde Shippe

Tel: (0492) 640013
On B5106

✕ lunchtime and evening

▨

⋈

🍺 Burtonwood Bitter

The spa village of Trefriw, notable for its chalybeate springs and its woollen mill (open to the public, who can view the whole process from raw wool to finished product), lies about a mile from Llanrwst, a notably friendly market town boasting an Inigo Jones bridge. Trefriw Spa, with its sulphurous waters, began life in 1863 when Lord Willoughby de Eresby built a small bath-house. Ten years later a rather grander pump room was constructed, and by the end of the nineteenth century customers were arriving by the boatload at Trefriw Quay. The boats stopped coming in 1939, and the spa ground to a halt in 1966. Not so the Olde Shippe, however. The oldest pub in the Conwy valley, dating from the sixteenth century, it has comfortably outlasted the spa and still makes an excellent base for walkers, pony trekkers, fishermen and – perhaps best of all – canoeists, who use the Conwy and its tributary the Afon Crafnant as well as nearby lakes such as Llyn Crafnant and Geirionnydd Lake. A memorial column by the latter commemorates the sixth-century poet Taliesin. The rather gloomy exterior of the Olde Shippe belies the warm welcome in the long bar; comfortable and cosy, offering excellent Burton-wood bitter and a wide array of decent and filling pub food.

TY CROES
Queen's Head

Tel: (0407) 810806
Bryn Du (half a mile from the A4080). OS345725

✗ lunchtime

🏠

🍺 **Burtonwood Bitter**

There are only a handful of pubs left in North Wales which serve ale direct from the cask, and the Queen's is one of them. Although it functions very much as a locals' pub, there are quite a few visitors to Anglesey who use it too, since it is not too far from the island's southern ring road, the A4080. To find it, take the turning opposite the Post Office in Llanfaelog (a British Rail sign indicates the way to Ty Croes station). The same family ran the pub as an unspoilt country inn for many years, and there were understandable fears when they finally gave it up that insensitive alterations would ruin it. But although some changes were made, and a pool table and one-armed bandit were introduced, there have been few other concessions to the late twentieth century, and the pub remains very largely unchanged. From the small entrance porch a wood-lined passageway leads to the central servery, where much of the available space is taken up by a row of metal casks of Burtonwood bitter. Hatchways from the servery open into the games room and a small lounge; and a separate room with a darts board leads off the passage. The floors are mainly flagged, and most of the ceilings are wood lined. An adequate range of bar food is served; live entertainment is regularly provided, and alongside the pub is a large beer garden.

Snowdonia

ARDDLIN
Horseshoe

Tel: (093 875) 318
On the B4392

✗ lunchtime and evening

🅱

☺

🅙

🍺 **Marston Burton Best Bitter, Pedigree**

Right at the junction of the B4392 and the busy A483 (the so-called Swansea to Manchester trunk road) a few miles north of Welshpool, the Horseshoe is a splendid place to break a long journey. Here all the family can relax, especially in the summer when the excellent garden, with its big and very popular adventure playground, and tables dotted amongst the trees, really comes into its own. The interior of the pub has been beautifully restored, rightly emphasising rather than destroying the essentially basic, rural style of the place, and in addition to an excellent bar with pub games including darts and dominoes there is a very welcome family room. The beers are well looked after and the range is widened to include regular guest beers in summer, while the food is appealingly simple and wholesome. The Shropshire Union canal runs close by – the little Guilsfield branch joins the main line at Burgedin Locks less than a mile away – with good coarse fishing and towpath walks. Also in the vicinity is Offa's Dyke and the long-distance footpath which provides a challenging walk along its course. Across the Severn valley the bizarre outline of the Breidden Hills meets the eye, with the Long Mountain to the east of Welshpool, its summit traversed by a Roman road, also well in view.

CASTLE
CAEREINION
Red Lion

Tel: (093 883) 233
On the B4385

✗ lunchtime and evening

🅱

☺

🅙

🍺 **Wood Parish Bitter; Draught Bass**

A growing but somewhat tucked-away village in the secluded Banwy (or Einion) valley, Castle Caereinion nevertheless has its own railway station – though admittedly it is on the narrow-gauge Welshpool and Llanfair Light Railway, which runs regular services between Llanfair Caereinion and Sylfaen. Half a mile from the station lies the Red Lion, its plain three-storey exterior dwarfed by the church spire behind but leading to a good village inn and a free house at that, with the excellent Parish Bitter from Wood's Brewery across the border in Shropshire the star of the show. A real mixture of styles can be found in the big open-plan bar, tastefully modernised but retaining its beautiful beamed ceiling. Solid timbers divide the bar into two distinct sections; the lounge area has high-backed settles, a red velvet window seat and solid wooden tables, while the main drinking area has a long low bench running into the inglenook fireplace, an impressive range of sports trophies, and – somewhat incongruously – cafe-style seating and formica tables near the entrance. To one side is the pool room, the haunt of many of the regulars and indeed of the landlord. There is also a somewhat rudimentary garden to one side of the pub. One small quibble: the music can be *very* intrusive at times.

LLANFAIR CAEREINION
Goat

Tel: (0938) 810428
High Street

✗ lunchtime and evening

🅱

🅰

📧

🍺 **Felinfoel Double Dragon; Welsh Brewers HB**

Opposite the prosperous-looking church and right in the centre of this big village, which aspires to but somehow just fails to achieve the status of a town, the Goat, trim, whitewashed and with a little porch guarding the entrance, presents a distinguished face to Llanfair's little High Street. The entrance hall leads straight to the stone-built bar, while to the right is a very pleasant lounge area with a big inglenook supported by a massive, fractured beam. All around here there are rather well-worn (and certainly well-used) easy chairs and settees, now creakily protesting somewhat, around low tables. The old country town hotel atmosphere is superb, precisely right for the unhurried enjoyment of a pint (especially a pint of Double Dragon!). The locals congregate here and in a rather more secluded lounge area further back into the pub, where there is also access to the enclosed garden at the rear. Through an archway to the left is the pool room, much used by Llanfair's younger pubgoers, and then, through another arch, a quieter bar. The bar menu is good value and relatively expansive in tone, with chicken dhansak a welcome replacement for the ubiquitous mild curry, for example, and the accommodation is well-regarded, as befits this excellent, characterful old inn.

Wynnstay Arms

Tel: (0938) 810203
Watergate Street

✗ lunchtime and evening

🍴

◉

⊨

🍺 **Ansells Mild, Tetley Bitter**

An imposing old pub on a street corner in the centre of Llanfair, the Wynnstay seems slightly faded outside but has a quite remarkable variety of rooms within. Amongst these is a separate restaurant with a good reputation locally, a pleasant, well-modernised lounge which opens out into an unexpectedly large red-carpeted function room, and a bar which is really excellent – cosy but comfortable, with a splendid inglenook and lots of brass, and popular amongst the domino-playing fraternity of the locality. Bed and breakfast is available, not least for those attracted by the narrow-gauge railway and then beguiled by the rolling countryside and sylvan little valleys in this well-hidden area. Families are easily accommodated in such a spacious pub, and there is also a pleasant garden around the corner. The Welshpool and Llanfair Light Railway, closed to passengers in 1930 but reopened by volunteers and now running regular steam-hauled services, has its terminus only half a mile away on the banks of the Banwy. Welshpool itself is worth visiting, especially for the Monday market, established by 1263 and still going strong in this borders town a mile from the majestic limestone and granite Powis Castle. Closer to home is a third worthwhile pub in Llanfair, the **Black Lion**, a former Wem Brewery pub which is once again many-roomed and welcoming.

LLANFIHANGEL-YNG-NGWYNFA
Goat

Tel: (069 184) 209
Off the B4382. OS080168

🍺 **Marston Border Exhibition, Border Bitter**

Probably the most difficult pub to find in the book, but a wonderfully unspoilt one. Detailed directions will not come amiss, especially to those doubtful of their ability to ask the way to Llanfihangel-yng-Ngwynfa, and all the more so because even those who locate this little village south of the brooding Berwyn Mountains could still fail to spot the pub itself. The simplest line of approach is to take the B4393 from Llanfyllin towards Llyn Efyrnwy (Lake Vrynwy), turn left into the narrow, twisting B4382, signposted to Dolanog, and turn left again onto the village street. The pub is on the right halfway up the street, though there is no pub sign – simply a little board above the porch with 'The Goat Inn' and a picture of a bewhiskered goat. It is a compact grey-rendered building, brightened somewhat by a couple of hanging baskets and by some michaelmas daisies in a border. Inside – and one can only get inside in the evenings, for the Goat doesn't open at lunchtime at all – the casual visitor will at first feel uncomfortable, for the approach to the bar appears to be through the living quarters. Embarassment will soon disappear, however, especially when the beer, fetched by jug from the cellar in the time-honoured way, begins to flow. It is a privilege to drink here, in a purist's pub virtually untouched by the relentless march of time.

LLANFYLLIN
Cain Valley
Hotel

Tel: (069 184) 366
High Street (A490)

✗ lunchtime and evening

≈

🍺 **Marston Pedigree; Sam Powell Original Bitter; Draught Bass**

A marvellous market town hotel, equally as good in its own way as the previous entry. The comparison doesn't end there, either, for this too was once known as the Goat Hotel, and at one time it was famous for its home-brewed Goat Ale, reputedly one of the best in a small, out-of-the-way town which formerly possessed a staggering (literally!) 43 pubs, many of them home-brew houses. After a period in the wilderness the Cain Valley commendably redis-covered real ale in the early 1970s, installing Bass together with Border Breweries' mild ale. The Bass survives, but the Border brewery, let alone the mild, has gone. Despite this, the hotel's hand-pumps continue to dispense a variety of excellent beers, from a range which changes slightly from time to time. Virtually at the end of the A490, the hotel, retaining the identity of a seventeenth-century coaching inn, has two smart lounge bars, with lots of oak beams and pillars, magnificent fireplaces, plenty of wood-panelling, and a series of unusual paintings together with several coats of arms and some old maps. Right at the back, and mainly catering for local drinkers, is a very different public bar. The Cain Valley is an excellent place to stay, too, both for its intrinsic qualities and for its location as a base for touring the Mid Wales countryside.

LLANGADFAN
Cann Office Hotel

Tel : (093 888) 203
On the A458

✕ lunchtime and evening

🍺

◎

🛏

🛢 **Marston Burton Best Bitter, Pedigree**

A rambling pub with quite a number of rooms, standing four-square on the main road, with two storeys and little black-and-white dormers. Traffic on the A458 roars past the front of the hotel, travelling from Welshpool to either Dolgellau or Machynlleth, but there is a calm air inside – and indeed in the large and very pleasant garden to the rear, sheltered by tall hedges. The public bar (where the handpumps are concealed, to the possible consternation of those ordering their beer elsewhere) is light and airy, with big solid wooden tables. Across the passageway is a little room with one-armed bandits, leading to the games room. Next is a pleasant, unfussy lounge where children are allowed and where lots of meals, including good value Sunday lunches, are served. And finally there is a small cocktail bar, not as exclusive as the name suggests but a nice, relaxing place for a quiet pint. The letting bedrooms are popular with walkers and fishermen – Glyndwr's Way runs close by, and the hotel has fishing rights on the Banwy, with its trout and grayling. Plenty of Welsh is spoken here, despite the closeness of the English border, but guests are soon made very welcome. A splendid old inn, well worth a visit.

LLANSANTFFRAID YM MECHAIN
Sun

Tel: (069 181) 214
On the A495

✗ lunchtime and evening

🍴

⊨

🍺 **Marston Border Exhibition, Border bitter, Pedigree**

Llansantffraid, a big low-lying village right by the Shropshire border south of Oswestry, and at the confluence of the rivers Efyrnwy and Cain as they near the River Severn, was once the home of Henry Jenks' Vyrnwy Brewery. Now the pubs sell Marston's beers from Burton-on-Trent, and a number of them operate largely as fishing hotels. The Sun is a particularly good-looking old inn, a long whitewashed two-storey building with lots of fuschias in flowering baskets along the verandah with its blue-painted benches. Food is a speciality at this friendly, unassuming village inn, with a separate restaurant as well as a good bar menu. The beer has great pulling power, too – as witness the crowd milling around outside at five to twelve on Sunday mornings! – and those who are simply here for the beer are not neglected, with a traditional public bar and neatly-furnished lounge at their disposal. Attractions in the area include the Tanat valley, with one of the most spectacular waterfalls in Wales, Pistyll Rhaedr above Llanrhaedr-ym-Mochnant, in one of its tributary valleys, and Offa's Dyke, the spectacular Dark Age earthwork thrown up to pen in the Welsh, with a good section on the western side of Llanymynech Hill.

MACHYNLLETH
Dyfi Forester

Tel: (0654) 2004
Heol y Doll (A487)

✘ lunchtime and evening

☺

⋈

⊕ **Marston Burton Best Bitter,
Pedigree**

Machynlleth, notable as the location of Glyndwr's Parliament in 1404 (the ancient stone building housing the Owain Glyndwr Institute is traditionally regarded as the meeting place) is a pleasant tourist centre with wide tree-lined streets. On the northern outskirts of the town centre, beyond the squat little parish church, the Dyfi Forester is a substantial three-storey black-and-white building dating from the 1870s. There is a single, nicely decorated U-shaped lounge bar, though it is neatly divided into a number of separate areas. Above the splendid fireplace is a fearsome looking antique gun, while a big brass plaque dominates another wall. The decorative emphasis is on fishing and wildfowling, appropriately enough in this market town not far from the head of the Dyfi estuary. Though the pub is a free house, the well-kept beer is from Marston's — simply because the proprietors have sought to bring added variety to the town. Downstairs there is a newly-opened bistro restaurant with an interesting menu including both traditional English and somewhat more unusual Danish specialities, including a mouth-watering Tivoli mixed platter based on herring slices. Across the river and into the trees (of the Dovey Forest) is the Centre for Alternative Technology, with a number of fascinating energy-saving projects on view.

Skinners Arms

Tel: (0654) 2354
Main Street (A487)

✘ lunchtime and evening

☺

⊕ **Burtonwood Bitter**

A stone's throw from the massive clock tower (erected in 1873 to mark the coming of age of Lord Castleragh) which dominates the centre of Machynlleth, the Skinners is a popular watering hole with a very welcoming atmosphere. Two-storey with dormers above, it is a typical town pub right on the main road, with an inn sign depicting Burtonwood's "top hat" trademark rather than the name of the pub. The small public bar, with its brick fireplace and half-timbering, has just a few bar stools and plenty of standing room for crowded evenings. The one-armed bandit is a little overpowering at first, however. On the other side of the island bar is the much larger lounge, with wooden tie-posts, a classic inglenook fireplace, festooned with brassware in its recesses, and plenty of wooden beams. Interesting photographs of old Machynlleth, a planned town of the thirteenth century, when it was granted a charter to hold a twice-yearly fair and weekly market, decorate the stone and half-timbered walls. Stools and bench seats are covered in greens and browns. The overall effect is tasteful and appealing. There is no garden – there simply isn't room in such an urban setting – but upstairs there is a family room, much appreciated as a useful extra feature of an excellent small town pub.

MANAFON
Beehive

Tel : (068 687) 244
On the B4390

✗ lunchtime and evening

⊗

☺

🍺 **Banks Mild, Bitter ; Whitbread Flowers IPA**

A smashing pub in a superb setting by the River Rhiw, one of the Severn's lesser-known tributaries, the Beehive has flourished since it was freed from the shackles of Greenall's Wem Brewery and is now a prosperous free house. It is a pub you have to make a special journey to visit – how many people would otherwise use the back road from Berriew to Tregynon? – but you won't regret it. Prominent by the roadside in the tiny village of Manafon, it is a very long, low white building on the left travelling westwards. The main bar area is very popular, especially with the dominoes fraternity, and there is also a splendid, comfortable area thick with trophies on the far side of an open brick fireplace of unusual design. Right at the end is the pool room. Even better, through a little doorway to the left of the entrance, is a delightful snug, ideal for a cosy chat – if only the piped music weren't so loud. The snug opens out through a beamed archway with 5ft 6ins headroom (you have been warned!) into a darts room which also has a secluded drinking area around two or three tables. The big garden behind the pub has a good selection of children's play equipment including swings and a monster slide. A really outstanding country pub, with the added attraction of Banks's beer too.

...ideal for a cosy chat.

PONTROBERT
Royal Oak

Tel: (093 884) 474
OS110127

✗ lunchtime and evening

🍴

⚓ Marston Pedigree

Occasionally described as "off the A495", the Royal Oak is a good mile and a half from the main road, tucked away in the peaceful and rather scattered village of Pontrobert. Set in lovely countryside, with delightful walks along the Efyrnwy valley – here beginning to widen out after a rocky journey from the deceptively peaceful reservoir of Llyn Efyrnwy – on either side of the old arched bridge in the centre of the village, it is an ideal spot to unwind. The Royal Oak helps in the unwinding, too, though Pedigree is now the only real ale on offer (Banks and Wadworth have featured in the past). It is a surprisingly large village pub with a variety of rooms, including a half-timbered public bar, with darts and dominoes, and a lounge decorated with horse brasses and with a somewhat subdued atmosphere. A second lounge, where children are welcome, is brighter and in demand as a dining room; big windows look down across the road to the Efyrnwy valley. An interesting and wide-ranging menu spans a much more catholic range than the usual bar snacks, and includes delicacies such as chicken tikka. Summer days can also be spent in the pub's pleasant garden, which caters well for children.

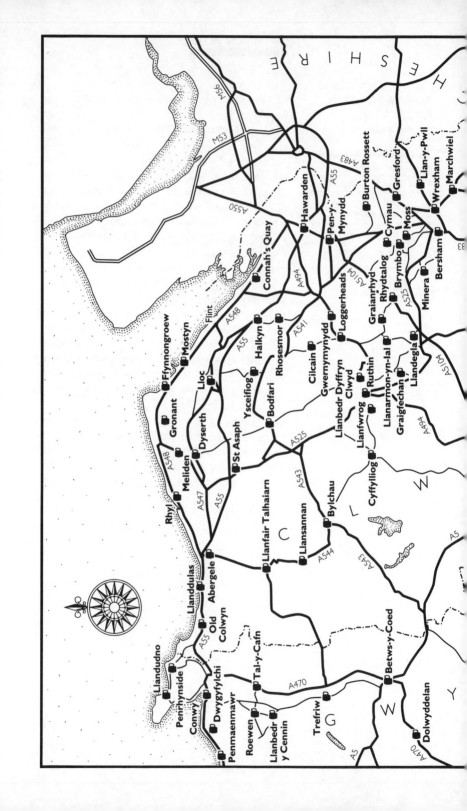

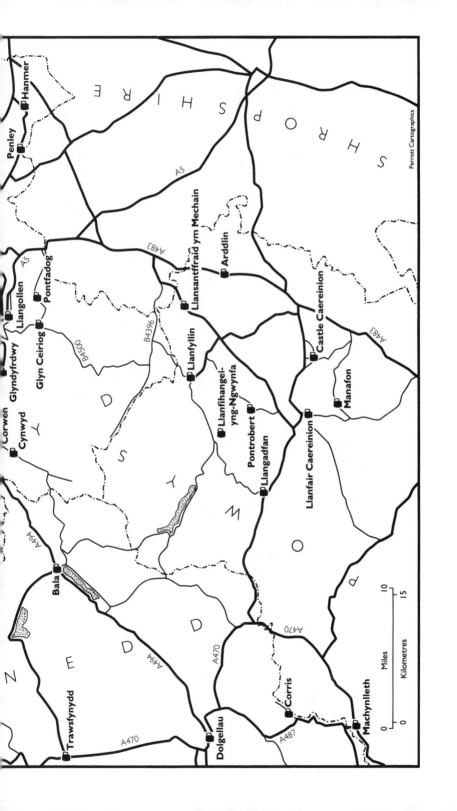

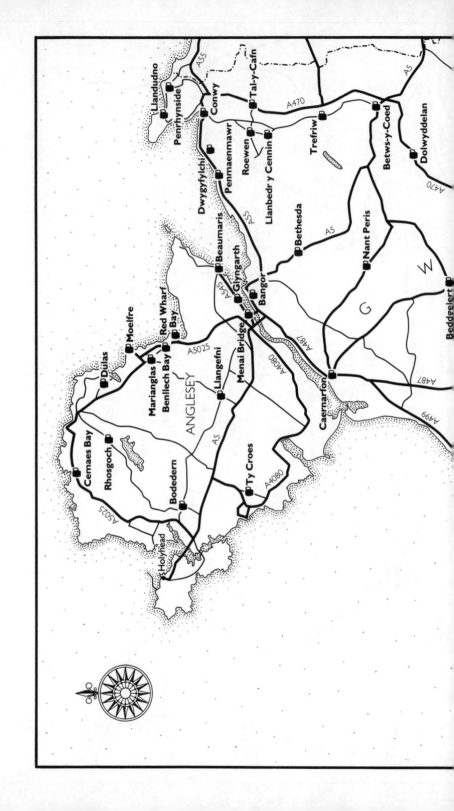

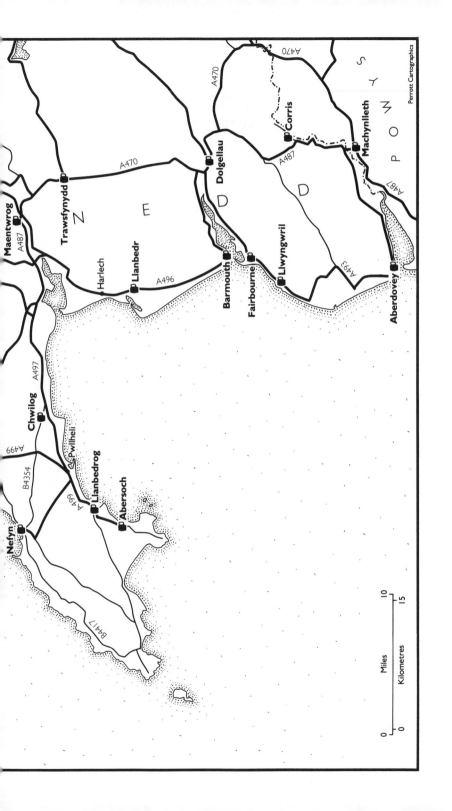

ALMA BOOKS

Alma Books Ltd is the publishing company set up by CAMRA (the Campaign for Real Ale) to produce titles of interest to pub-lovers, beer-drinkers, tourists and travellers.

For more information about Alma Books and to obtain the books listed below (which are also available at all good bookshops), write to Alma Books Ltd., 34 Alma Road, St. Albans, Herts. AL1 3BW.

Available now:

The Best Pubs in Devon and Cornwall	**£4.95**
The Best Pubs in East Anglia	**£4.95**
The Best Pubs in Lakeland	**£3.95**
The Best Pubs in London	**£4.95**
The Best Pubs in Yorkshire	**£4.95**

Companion volumes to the North Wales guide offering the reader detailed descriptions of the finest pubs in the area.

Good Pub Food **£5.95**

Over four hundred pubs around the country where good food is as much a priority as good beer and you may find some of the best examples of traditional British cooking, using the finest local produce.

The Best Pubs for Families **£4.95**

A completely updated nationwide listing of pubs which serve real ale, where children are not just tolerated, but really made welcome by providing good facilities including meals and play areas (indoors as well as outside).

Forthcoming attractions:
A Bedside Book of Beer
The Great British Pub

Join CAMRA

If you like good beer and good pubs you could be helping in the fight to preserve, protect and promote them. CAMRA was set up in the early seventies to fight against the mass destruction of a part of Britain's heritage.

The giant brewers are still pushing through takeovers, mergers and closures of their smaller regional rivals. They are still reducing the availability and diluting the quality of a magnificent and uniquely British product – real ale. They are still trying to impose national brands of beer and lager on their customers whether they like it or not, and they are still closing down town and village local pubs or converting them into grotesque 'theme' bars.

CAMRA wants to see genuine free competition in the brewing industry, fair prices, civilised licensing laws, and, above all, a top quality product brewed by local breweries in accordance with local tastes, and served in pubs that maintain the best features of a tradition that goes back centuries.

If you are in sympathy with these aims you could be expressing that sympathy in a positive way, by joining CAMRA. We have well over 20,000 members and that's not including our three fully paid-up dogs and two cats! Yet we're pitting ourselves against the power and financial muscle of a multi-million pound, multi-national industry. We need active campaigning members, but we are also grateful for the support of people whose only involvement may be to pay their membership subscription once a year. It's only £9, but each additional subscription helps us to campaign that bit more effectively across the whole spectrum of pub issues on behalf of *all* pub-users.

If you leave it to others, you may wake up one day to find *your* local pub shut, *your* local brewery closed down, *your* favourite beer no longer being brewed. So join CAMRA and help us to prove that the most important person in the brewing industry isn't the megalomaniac chairman of some brewing giant, but that most vital, and under-valued person – the pub customer.

Full membership £9 Joint husband/wife membership £9 Life membership £90 I/We wish to become members of CAMRA Ltd. I/We agree to abide by the memorandum and articles of association of the company. I/We enclose a cheque/p.o. for £9/£90.

Name(s) _____

_____

_____

Address _____

_____

_____

Signature(s)

_____

CORRECTIONS AND AMENDMENTS

Every year sees many Welsh pubs changing hands. A new licensee can bring improvements or disaster to even the finest establishment. While most details were checked shortly before going to press, errors will inevitably occur and changes come thick and fast.

If you come upon listed pubs which have been ruined or if you find an undiscovered gem on your travels, let me know and I will investigate for the next edition.

Complete the form below or write to: Mike Dunn (North Wales), Alma Books, 34 Alma Road, St. Albans, Hertfordshire, AL1 3BW.

County _____

Town or village _____

Name of pub _____

Address _____

Location (A or B road) _____

Tel no. _____ Name of licensee _____

Description of pub (including bars, food, family room and any special facilities)

_____

_____

Beers _____

_____

_____

Reasons for recommendation for inclusion in/deletion from the guide

_____

_____

Your name and address _____

_____

_____

Postcode _____

INDEX